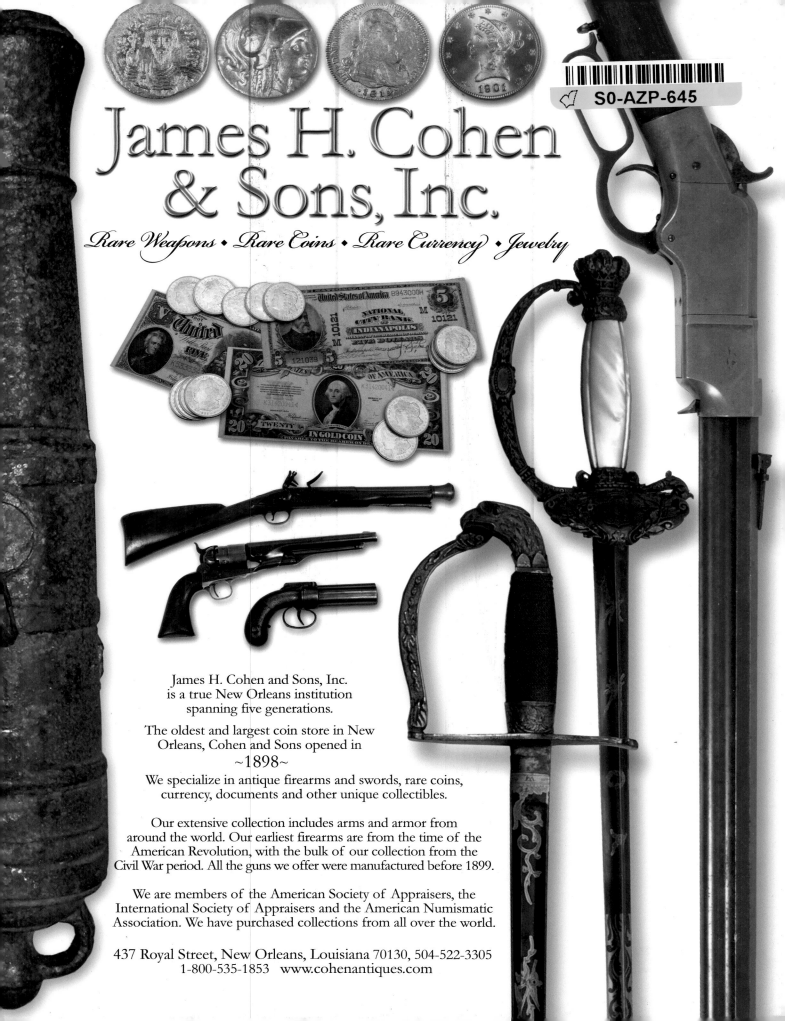

# James H. Cohen & Sons, Inc.

*Rare Weapons • Rare Coins • Rare Currency • Jewelry*

James H. Cohen and Sons, Inc. is a true New Orleans institution spanning five generations.

The oldest and largest coin store in New Orleans, Cohen and Sons opened in ~1898~

We specialize in antique firearms and swords, rare coins, currency, documents and other unique collectibles.

Our extensive collection includes arms and armor from around the world. Our earliest firearms are from the time of the American Revolution, with the bulk of our collection from the Civil War period. All the guns we offer were manufactured before 1899.

We are members of the American Society of Appraisers, the International Society of Appraisers and the American Numismatic Association. We have purchased collections from all over the world.

437 Royal Street, New Orleans, Louisiana 70130, 504-522-3305
1-800-535-1853   www.cohenantiques.com

# Contents

Published by Gris Gris Publications
Photography and Text by Todd and April Fell
Computer Graphic Artist Ashley Fell

First Printing 2004
Second Edition Copyright © 2009 - All rights reserved

Photographs pages 56 & 57 by Infrogmation,
CC Attribution License 2.5

Regal Printing, Ltd. -  Printed in Hong Kong

*N*ew Orleans is intriguing, bawdy, mysterious and exciting. Her exotic history has been the colorful story of explorers and exiles, patriots and pirates, Voodoo Queens and Mardi Gras Kings, African slaves and European aristocrats, of Southern genteel attitudes and Yankee business savvy.

Her people have struggled against difficult hardships and reveled in the pleasures of food and drink, Carnival and celebration – *les bons temps roulez !* New Orleans' complex personality was born of diverse cultures, and left a legacy of tenacious tradition, unusual language, distinctive architecture and unique customs.

New Orleans was the birthplace of Jazz and creator of its own world renowned Creole Cuisine. It is called "The Crescent City," "The City that Care Forgot," "The Big Easy," and "America's Most Interesting City."

*Above: "Along Royal Street," by George Pearce*
*Left: Publisher Todd Fell planning a photograph of a New Orleans architectural treasure*

La Nouvelle Orleans

In 1718, to protect the Mississippi
for France, French Canadian
explorer Sieur de Bienville,
founded New Orleans

La Salle had laid claim for France to all the lands along the Mississippi River in 1682, but a capital city was needed, near the mouth of the river, to protect French claims against British and Spanish competition in the New World.

Bienville had his architect lay out the grid of streets that form the present French Quarter, and crude huts and a little wooden levee were erected on the swampy soil. Despite the continual hardships of sickness, hurricanes and the ever flooding river, as well as conflict and corruption within the colony, the tiny settlement grew into a little city during the early 1700's.

The strange mix of settlers included French aristocrats, soldiers, professionals and speculators, as well as shiploads of undesirables, sent from the jails of Paris. Ursuline Nuns arrived to care for the little community and soon began looking after the "Casket Girls" (poor, but proper girls, sent to become wives for the settlers).

German farmers suffered the difficulties of clearing land, near the town. In 1755, the Acadians, ancestors of today's "Cajuns," began arriving in the colony, mostly settling away from city life, as trappers and fisher-

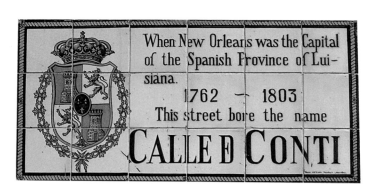

When New Orleans was the Capital of the Spanish Province of Luisiana. 1762 – 1803 This street bore the name CALLE D CONTI

men, in the marshy lands nearby. For more than a century, there was the continuous arrival of slaves from Africa and the West Indies. The "People of color," both free and slave, made great contributions to the unique culture of the city.

In 1762, French King Louis XV, gave Louisiana to his cousin, Charles III, of Spain. Deserted by France, and with no interest in becoming Spanish, the unhappy colonists began discussing the formation of a republic. The first Spanish officials who came were sent packing, but romantic ideas of independence ended abruptly, when Alexander O'Reilly arrived with 3,000 soldiers to rule the colony for Spain. Executing the leading French patriots, he became known as "Bloody O'Reilly." But the colonists adjusted quickly to the consistency of Spanish rule and the inter-marriage between Spanish and French became common. Children born in the colony were called "Creoles," a term also applied to the culture and cuisine that developed in this colonial community.

A terrible fire swept New Orleans in 1788, destroying 856 of the original French buildings. Six years later, another fire took

200 of the new structures. Gov. Carondelet decreed that all subsequent construction be of brick, with slate and tile roofs, to prevent future disasters. The new architecture was of mostly Spanish style, with the arches and walled courtyards seen today.

During the 1790's, Santo Dominicans, escaping an uprising on their Caribbean island, sailed to New Orleans. These were French speaking, educated émigrés, who brought with them their art, music, theater, schools and energetic spirit.

In 1803, representatives from Spain, France and the United States met in the city. Papers were signed completing the secret 1801 transfer of Louisiana from Spain back to France, and then Napoleon's sale of

Louisiana to the United States. The New Orleanians felt that they had been betrayed again – this time, left to the "barbarians," since the tough, rowdy and uncultured riverboat men were the only Americans most Creoles had ever seen. They did not make the newcomers welcome.

The mostly Puritan Anglos, who began streaming into the city, found the Catholic Creole society "closed" to them, and, disapproving of the Creole lifestyle, they began building their own community on the other side of Canal Street. Competition and differences were temporarily put aside by the common effort to defeat the British in the Battle of New Orleans in 1815 (the last conflict of the War of 1812). But, for the

*Right: The St. Louis Cathedral*

*It became common for Spanish soldiers to change their surnames to those of their French brides. Many German names were changed to be French, by officials of the colony.*

most part, the Vieux Carré remained the old, Creole, French speaking section, while a "new," English speaking, American city spread up river from it.

The successful granulation of sugar on a nearby plantation had begun the enormous sugar cane industry. This, coupled with the arrival of the first Mississippi steamboat in 1812, ushered in the beginnings of the "Golden Age" for New Orleans. She now became the commercial hub for the entire Mississippi Valley and port to the world.

The years between 1830 and the Civil War brought unprecedented wealth to the city. The "Americans" made fortunes by brokering, financing and shipping goods through the port. They built grand houses along Coliseum Square and then formed the City of Lafayette, and within it the Garden District. The Creoles' wealth was tied to the sugar plantations. In the Vieux Carré, planters built grand town houses next door to successful merchants, bankers and lawyers.

This was the time of elegant balls, extravagant entertainment and lavish decor. Furniture, building materials and fashions were imported from Europe. The French opera and theaters were packed. Gentlemen studied with fencing masters and sent their children for education in France. The city was the wealthiest in the United States!

New Orleans' unique history had already produced a lifestyle of contradictions - strict codes of chivalry, strong religion, obsession with family honor and tradition, side by side with every form of pleasure seeking and extravagance, of superstition and vice.

Gambling had always been a common past time in the city, both among wealthy aristocratic gentlemen and rough river front bar crowds. Governed by a code of honor, cards and dice caused many a suicide, duel or loss of family fortune. Whole plantations were even won and lost at gaming tables.

In 1847, New Orleans was the leading horse racing center in the United States, boasting four racetracks. There was also betting on cockfights, prizefights, and battles staged between various animals.

In the hundred years before the Civil War, chivalrous pride and family honor had led to countless duels. Though the practice was always illegal, as many as ten duels were fought on any Sunday morning and as often between friends, as strangers.

Voodoo had come to the Colony in the 1700's, with the slaves brought in from the West Indies. Though the Creole population was always strictly Roman Catholic, and the Americans devout in their Christianity, the use of Voodoo power to add a little influence in matters, was common practice.

Perhaps the strangest of these unique

9

Right: "Steamboat Passengers," by Walter Stewart

Below: "A Creole Gentleman," 1833 (Antoine Meffre Rouzan, a free-man-of-color, who called himself, a "Creole of color") courtesy, Louisiana State Museum

cultural practices were the Quadroon Balls. These evenings were held for young white "gentlemen" to meet young Quadroon girls (one fourth Negro) from whom to choose a mistress. Many a New Orleans "gentleman" provided for two homes (and families), one with his acknowledged white wife and one with his secret Quadroon mistress.

But the wealth of the city's Golden Age was based on river commerce and slave labor, both of which were halted abruptly by the Civil War. Occupation by Federal troops lasted 15 years and was witness to constant riots, corruption, impeachments and battles in the streets. For a few months there were even two governors and two state legislatures in New Orleans!

The huge numbers of slaves, never having shared in the prosperity before the war, were now expected to find a new place within the commercial, political and social life of the city. The rapid rise of the railroads after the war, spelled the end of the tremendous commerce that had once jammed the river. There was no returning to the Antebellum days.

White Creoles and Americans shared in their common defeat and loss. Together, as

*"Creole" meant someone of French or Spanish parents who was born in the colony.. It was applied to white people, born in New Orleans, and the culture they developed. But it was also used by the "free persons of color" (usually of mixed heritage - often of French fathers and usually French Creole in culture), whose descendants in New Orleans, still call themselves Creoles.*

Left: The Steamboat
"J.M. White," by
John Stobart

Below: View of
Canal Street,
in 1910

*The word "Creole" has often caused confusion. Besides the question of "mixed" or "white," the word was also used in the first two centuries, to describe the dialect spoken by the African slaves under the French domination. Today, it is used most often in reference to the famous cuisine of the city.*

"Southerners," they found strength in their traditions, heroes and culture. The resentments of Reconstruction replaced slavery with the insidious system of segregation.

In the years following Reconstruction, corruption and vice grew even more prevalent. By 1880, gambling, prostitution, crime, political payoffs and corrupt police had created desperate cries for reform. Finally in 1897, a plan was devised for the creation of two "districts," for all illegal activities (to control them). But instead of curbing these activities, "Storyville," as the district near the French Quarter was called, became "a spectacle of legalized vice," and a major tourist attraction for the city. Its fancy "sporting palaces" offered "entertainment" of all kinds for gentlemen. It thrived until it was closed and torn down in 1917.

Most people regard New Orleans as the birthplace of Jazz, and all agree that it prospered in Storyville, where black musicians entertained in the palaces. After Storyville closed, some of these Jazz artists went north. But many Jazz musicians remained, black and white, and their improvisational art form thrived in the city of its birth.

During the 19th and early 20th centuries,

New Orleans received large numbers of immigrants from Ireland and then Italy (mostly Catholic, like the Creoles). The customs, cuisine and aspirations they brought with them, blended into the already complex and colorful culture of the city.

Being built on a swamp, with heavy rain fall, between a great river and a large lake, annual floods and epidemics had cost lives and property every year. The city had continually built all types of levees. But a major effort in the early 1900's included the installation of enormous pumps under the "neutral grounds" of most major avenues (still in use today to divert the constant excess rain water into the lake). Countless open ditches and cisterns were eliminated as well. These efforts successfully stopped most flooding (in the old parts of the city) and eliminated the deadly annual epidemics.

By the turn of the 20th Century, many Creoles had lost their fortunes or moved along Esplanade Ave. Their once elegant Vieux Carré homes became tenements for the new immigrants, who were settling there (with clotheslines strung across the ornate balconies). Some buildings were crumbling from neglect.

11

999 PLAYING CARDS STEAMBOAT

It was mostly writers and artists who rediscovered the Vieux Carré, as a picturesque place to live and work. During the 1920's, a Bohemian community developed, as the old buildings were sketched, painted and written about, rented as studios or bought for restoration. The Vieux Carré Commission, established in 1936, has successfully blocked most attempts to modernize, alter or tear down the old architecture.

Most of the fine old homes of the Garden District have been preserved. While some mansions on St. Charles and Esplanade have been lost, there remains an enormous display of architectural treasures to provide us with a glimpse into another time.

New Orleans today, has all the problems of a large, modern city, but, uniting the people from all backgrounds, is the rich legacy they share - of their distinctive traditions, customs and history, of their music, cuisine and architecture, and of the pride in their uniqueness among American cities.

*The narrow streets of the French Quarter, form a living museum, where history can be studied in the legends, the unusual traditions and the brick and cypress of the weathered buildings.*

*Above:
Jackson Square,
showing the
St. Louis Cathedral,
the Presbytere and
the sculpture of
Andrew Jackson,
by Clark Mills*

Come, let us begin where the little colony began, at the old Place d'Armes, now called Jackson Square. The heart of the original settlement, this was the parade ground for the soldiers, surrounded by their government and religious buildings. It was here that citizens gathered for the raising of eight different flags. Here, they congregated for celebrations, executions and calamities. Here, they welcomed distinguished visitors and watched the continuous arrival of ships, bearing immigrants from many countries and differing stations in life.

Dominating the Square is the St. Louis Cathedral, the oldest cathedral in the United States. When the Parish Church (built in 1727) burned in the great fire of 1788, it was replaced by the St. Louis Cathedral, a gift to the city from Don Almonester y Roxas. Having come to the colony from Spain as a penniless notary, in just 20 years, he had amassed sufficient fortune and prestige to be the city's benefactor. In addition to the Cathedral, he financed several other public buildings.

Escaping destruction in the fire of 1794, the Cathedral was dedicated that year – a smaller building than it is presently, with rounded Spanish style bell towers. In 1849, it was rebuilt to be larger and "more French," with the towers taller and pointed, as they are today.

Though the outside appears rather modest, the interior is well worth a visit, with dramatic murals, sculpture, stained glass and the inscribed marble tombs of early prominent citizens (including Don Almonester).

To the left of the Cathedral stands the

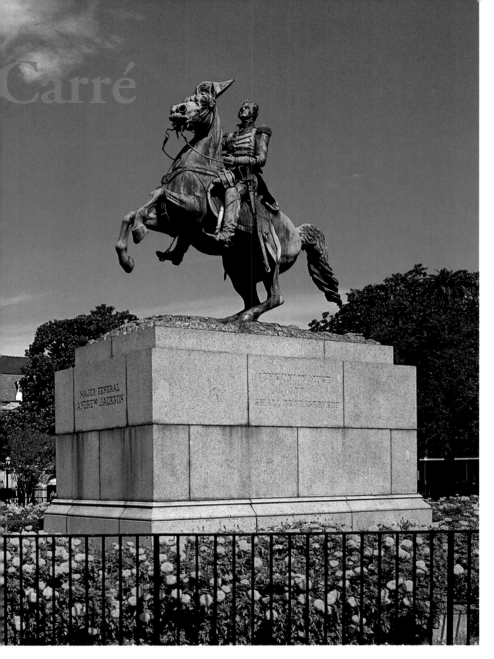

Cabildo. A French government building was here when the Spanish took power and they used it for their "Casa Capitular," or Capital House. Here, the Spanish governing council met, called the "Very Illustrious Cabildo." Destroyed in the great fire, the building was replaced with the new Spanish structure, which in turn, was damaged in the fire of 1794. The remains of the previous walls were incorporated in its reconstruction.

In 1803, papers were signed in the Cabildo, for the transfer of Louisiana from Spain back to France, and the Louisiana Purchase, 20 days later, which almost doubled the size of the United States. New Orleans, as an American city, used the Cabildo as its City Hall. The mansard roof was added in 1847, and, soon after, the Louisiana Supreme Court moved in,

occupying the building until 1911. It was then made part of the Louisiana State Museum.

In 1988, the Cabildo had another serious fire and all types of volunteers worked together heroically to save the artifacts and archives of the museum. The building was restored soon after.

To the right of the Cathedral is the Presbytere, designed to be the rectory for the Cathedral. Only the first floor of the Presbytere had been built, when the 1794 fire destroyed the Cabildo. The necessity to rebuild the government house put a stop to the rectory construction.

In 1813, the building was finally completed and the Louisiana State Courts moved in. The Presbytere received its mansard roof in 1847 and in 1911, became part of the Louisiana State Museum.

*Important visitors to New Orleans were sometimes housed at the Cabildo. In 1825, "royal" quarters were prepared for the visit of the American Revolutionary hero, the Marquis de Lafayette. In very different style, in 1814, Pierre Laffite was jailed, in one of the cells in the rear of the building.*

*Above: The Presbytere*

*Above: One of the many tile plaques throughout the French Quarter which explain what the streets were called during the Spanish years.*

When New Orleans was the Capital of the Spanish Province of Luisiana.
1762 — 1803
This square bore the name
PLAZA D ARMAS

The little iron submarine, which stood until 1999 at the Presbytere, was moved to a lab to be studied and preserved. Believed for years to be the "Pioneer," the first Confederate sub, it is now known not to be, and its identity is currently a mystery.

The two handsome red brick structures that border Jackson Square are the Pontalba Buildings. They were built by the Baroness Pontalba in 1851 to be fashionable apartments, above ground floor businesses, as they still are today. One apartment, "The 1850 House," was restored and furnished, to show that period to the public.

The initials "A P," woven into the cast iron railing of the Pontalba Buildings, stand for the families of Almonester and Pontalba. Micaela, Don Almonester's daughter, was only two when the old Don died. When she was 16, her mother arranged her marriage to her cousin Celestin, son of Baron Joseph Xavier de Pontalba. Two of the richest families in the colony could arrange a marriage, but they could not arrange its happiness. When the headstrong Micaela left her husband, her domineering father-in-law made threats against her. The tensions grew, until one day, in France, the old Baron drew two pistols, shooting Micaela and then himself.

He died, but she recovered and returned to New Orleans.

Upon her return (during the 1840's) the Baroness was distressed to find that the vibrant "American" section of the city was drawing business away from her Vieux Carré. She felt that a "modernized" and beautified public square might re-attract commerce to the old Creole section. By 1851, she had been the impetus for putting mansard roofs on the Cabildo and Presbytere, rebuilding the Cathedral to be "more French," constructing the Pontalba buildings, adding the handsome iron gates and fence to the old Place d'Armes, and commissioning the statue of Andrew Jackson as the centerpiece for her "new" Jackson Square.

The statue of Andrew Jackson, hero of the Battle of New Orleans, was made by Clark Mills. The inscription on its base, "The Union Must and Shall be Preserved," was ordered engraved by occupying Union General Ben Butler, during the Civil War.

A New Orleans tradition surrounds Jackson Square, in the form of the many artists, busy painting and sketching. To work on the Square, artists must have a license and sell only "original" art (nothing printed or reproduced). Portraits, Vieux Carré scenes and caricatures are the most popular works. Often entertainers and musicians also vie for the tourists' attention.

Behind the Cathedral is the peaceful St.

*The art of "parfum" in New Orleans, is part of the French heritage. At Bourbon French Parfum, the art has been passed, in the same family, since the shop opened in 1843. At Hové Parfum, these skills have come down from French Creole great grand mother to the current generation.*

Anthony's Garden (or Cathedral Garden).
Père Antoine was a priest in the Cathedral
for almost fifty years, performing the
baptisms, weddings and funerals for most
of the families in the Vieux Carré. Though
he came to the colony from Spain in 1779,
as Fray Antonio de Sedella, he became so
loved by the community, that he was
known by the French name, Père Antoine,
(but the garden was given the *English*
version of the name, Anthony).

With sandaled feet and a coarse, brown
monk's robe, he led a simple life, giving
most of his salary to the needy. Though a
continual thorn in the side of his superiors
(he was once expelled from the colony for
insubordination) he had a large, enthusiastic
following of Parishioners and non Catholics
alike.

In the Garden is a monument dedicated
to some of those who gave their lives,
trying to give aid in one of New Orleans'
terrible yellow fever epidemics. The worst
took 11,000 lives in 1853. Each year, many
who could afford to, took their families,
and went to a plantation or to another city,
to avoid the epidemics. Many times the city
was quarantined from the rest of the
country, and the desperately needed supplies, aid workers and food became almost
impossible to bring in. But money and
courageous volunteers *did* get through each
year, from other parts of the country, to
help relieve the suffering.

During this period, most houses in the
city had huge cisterns behind them to catch
rain water. In 1905, when it was discovered
that the mosquito, which caused yellow
fever, bred its young in this standing household water supply, the city energetically
undertook the enormous task of eliminating
all cisterns and other standing water, while
building a municipal water system. It also
rid itself of most of its rats, which were
spreading other diseases.

*Right: Dr. Thomas House, 626 Pirates' Alley*

*Below: Faulkner House, 624 Pirates' Alley*

*When Dr. Joseph Martin built the mansion at 709 Royal, he signed the contract with the builder for a total price of $6,918.*

*Below: "Pirates' Alley" by George Pearce, artist of the 1930's*

Along the garden, behind the Cabildo, lies a narrow and picturesque passage known as "Pirates' Alley." There are many theories as to the origin of its name, but it has long been a favorite romantic setting for artists, writers and quiet walks.

On the Alley, at 624, is the house where William Faulkner (1929 Nobel Prize winner) lived in a small rented apartment. Here he wrote his first novel, *Soldier's Pay*, in 1925. He also wrote many articles about his experiences in New Orleans.

The tall house, at 626, was built with only two stories in 1823, by a prominent physician, Dr Pierre Frederic Thomas. (The upper floors were not added until around 1870.) It is different from its neighbors, which were all part of a row of eleven identical buildings (with arched doorways) constructed in the 1830's by Melasie La Branche, widow of a wealthy German sugar planter. The buildings wrap around from Pirates' Alley, along Royal and onto St. Peter. They have each been altered by their different owners, over the years.

The Garden and Pirates' Alley both end

*"Galleries" (as the French called them) are wider than "balconies" and have supporting pillars to the ground, so that the sidewalks ("banquettes") are protected from the sun and rain. "Balconies" are narrower and are supported on the building, itself.*

single floor house of a well known notary, Pedro Pedesclaux. Financial difficulties forced him to sell to partners, Dr. Ives LeMonnier and Pharmacist François Grandchamps, in 1811. The new owners rented out the ground floor and added two stories to be the doctor's residence. The doctor was living here when he joined Andrew Jackson's forces in 1814, for the Battle of New Orleans. LeMonnier's initials can be seen in the graceful wrought iron of the balconies. When the fourth floor was added in 1876, neighbors feared that the swampy soil would not support its height.

A small A&P grocery store occupied the opposite corner at 701 Royal for years. The building was erected soon after 1789 and was a bakery in the early years, with ovens and a great smokestack behind it. Cadet Molon's bread was prized by Creole households, but it was enjoyed by many of the poor, as well. The goodhearted baker accepted a kind of "food stamp," issued by Père Antoine, and he gave the priest much of his "second day" bread for distribution among the poor.

In 1791, a troupe of actors from Santo Domingo created New Orleans' first theater, *The Tabary*, at 730 St. Peter. Performances were in French – very political and often very rowdy. The Spanish authorities repeatedly shut it down. In 1806, it reopened its doors as *The Spectacle*, and offered a variety of plays in French. The Theater burned in 1816 and the present home was erected in 1825.

The house at 714 St. Peter was a typical residence of its period, with courtyard and a picturesque staircase. It originally had a red tile roof. Built in 1829 for Dr. Ives Le Monnier, it was sold in 1838 to become the town house of George Raymond Locoul, a prosperous sugar planter.

Across the street, the house at 717 was bought in 1811 by the very wealthy Bartholome Camponel, a "free man of color" who lived in Paris part of the year.

Don Francisco Collel, a captain in the Spanish Regiment, built the handsome home at 718 in 1792. In 1806, it became the

*Center: The Skyscraper or House of Sieur George, 640 Royal*

*Below: LaBranche House, 700 Royal. Monsieur LaBranche was actually a German, of the name, "Zweig" (meaning twig). His name was changed to LaBranche by French authorities, a common French practice with German names. For many New Orleanians, there is little trace of their German heritage*

*"Wrought" iron (the hot metal shaped and hammered by a black smith) was used in all of the original metal balconies and galleries.*
*During the 1850's, "cast" iron (formed in a mold) became popular and many ornate cast railings were added to buildings, often replacing original wrought iron.*

*In the time before either air conditioning or television, balconies and galleries served as more than decor. They gave protection to the tall French windows, opened for ventilation in the hot climate, and allowed enjoyment of the activities in the street below.*

in Royal Street (Rue Royale), which was the "Main Street" of the Vieux Carré, and perhaps displays more ornate ironwork, than any other street in the Quarter.

Some of the more picturesque cast iron along Royal is at 700, the corner LaBranche House, with its lacy pattern of acorns and oak leaves. These galleries were added to the house during the 1850's.

Across at 640 Royal, stands a different looking building, known both as the "House of Sieur George" (from a George Washington Cable story that was set here) and "The Skyscraper." It was originally the

*Above: Old
Preservation Hall,
726 St. Peter*

*Left: Rounded
cypress railings
at 637 Royal*

*A "carriage way"
is the large entrance
to a building, for
carriages to pass
from the street to
the courtyard or
stable behind.
Often arched,
they usually have
a gate or large
door. A small,
"pedestrian" door,
sometimes cut in
the larger door, is
called a "wicket."*

town house of a prominent planter, Etienne de Flechier. In 1933, Pat O'Brien opened his popular nightclub here.

Preservation Hall is the wonderfully picturesque old building at 726 St. Peter. It was constructed (with its ornate wrought iron gates) in 1817. Since 1961, it has been the home of traditional New Orleans Jazz, played by many of the old time greats and those who have learned under them.

The house at 638 Royal still has its original curved cypress balcony railings on two floors, which extend along the side of the building over a passageway to the back.

In the early 1800's, Zenon Cavelier and his brother Antoine ran a mercantile business at 627 Royal. Their father had run the business here since 1777, but his building had burned in the 1788 fire, and had been replaced with this one soon after.

In 1860, the building was home to the "golden voiced songbird" Angelina Patti. At only 17, she was a sensation at the newly opened French Opera House that season, and soon had gentlemen pacing the street in front of the house, hoping to catch a glimpse of the visiting star.

A French merchant, who came to New Orleans in 1781, Jean Baptiste Labatut built a small house at 623 Royal. Attorney Gen-

eral of "The Illustrious Cabildo" during the Spanish period, he also served as a general in the Battle of New Orleans. The Labatuts hosted many important visitors and elegant social affairs. In 1821, they rebuilt their old home to be two tall twin houses. (photo, page 35)

They rented the twin of their new house (at 621 Royal) to a lawyer, Alexandre Graihle, in the 1830's. The Graihle's home was also the setting for lavish entertaining. But Mr. Graihle is remembered more for the two duels he fought with the fiery old, well known Creole, Bernard de Marigny (who already had 15 successful duels to his credit when the lawyer challenged him). Graihle, whose honor had been injured in both "affairs d'honeur," was also the one whose body was injured both times.

In the 1840's, the Graihle's house became home to the daughter of General Zachary Taylor. "Old Rough and Ready" had his home near Baton Rouge, and often visited his daughter and her husband. His success in the War with Mexico had made him a hero in New Orleans. In 1847, he was given a huge celebration, complete with a triumphal arch erected in the Place d'Armes. He was elected U.S. President in 1848 and died in office in 1850.

*Right: Tennessee Williams House, 720 Toulouse*

*Below: Nicolas House, 723 Toulouse*

*"Slave Quarters" are the "half houses," seen behind, or as a wing of a main house. They usually housed the servants on the upper floors, while the stables and kitchens were on the ground floor by the courtyard. Today, slave quarter apartments are often considered very desirable.*

In a home at 615 Royal, two different French governors of the colony had lived before it was lost in the great fire. In 1832, Zenon Cavelier, then the president of the Banque d'Orleans, erected the present building and its twin at 611. The house has one of the largest "slave quarters" in the city, said to have housed 37 servants at one time. The popular restaurant that now uses the enormous courtyard for outdoor dining, took its name from the sisters, Emma and Bertha Camors, who ran a variety store here from 1886 to 1906.

Next door, 611 was the home of Gov. André Roman, a prominent sugar planter and twice Governor of Louisiana. Host of many brilliant social gatherings, he gave a grand dinner party in 1837 for John James Audubon and was instrumental in getting the State to purchase *Birds of North America.*

In 1831, the son of Gen. Labatut built twin houses, across the street from his parents. A notable law office occupied the first floor of 624, and Dr. Isidore Labatut and his wife entertained Creole aristocracy in their home above. Their descendants lived in the house for more than a century.

The next door twin, at 616, has always been admired for its handsome courtyard.

In the 1840's, another prominent doctor, Auguste Ferrier, lived here. When his daughter made her debut, so many guests accepted their invitation, that the adjoining Labatut house was "borrowed" for the evening. The ironwork was removed so that guests could pass from one balcony to the other, as if it were one huge house.

The house at 622 Royal was built in 1811, and sold to John Grymes in 1826. He was the District Attorney, well respected, and a friend of Gov. Claiborne. When the Governor arrested Pierre Laffite, Grymes caused a sensation, when he gave up his prominent post to become attorney for the Laffites (the famous "pirate" smugglers). Grymes later married Governor Claiborne's widow.

Dr. Germain Ducatel (who had fought in the Battle of New Orleans) retired from practice in 1825. He built the adjoining structures at 600 Royal and opened a popular dry goods store in the corner one.

The three buildings at 601 Royal (and 707 Toulouse) were constructed in 1834 by Nicolas Brigot, a wealthy merchant. Among the many tenants who lived in the upstairs apartments, was Denis Prieur, six term Mayor of New Orleans, from 1828 to 1838

*Above: Brigot Buildings, 707 Toulouse There are still many reminders of times past, painted on walls throughout the French Quarter.*

*Right: Courtyard of the Maison de Ville Hotel, 727 Toulouse*

ed. Built in 1798, this was the "Casa
cio," of Jean François Merieult, a
merchant and junior judge in the
ious Cabildo." In 1819, it was sold to
nan merchant and banker, Vincente
who financed the paving of Royal
It was later the home of La Banque
sociation (a bank that lent mostly to
lanters).

oldest house on Royal Street stands
having survived the fire of 1794 that
ed most of its neighbors. (picture,
) Built by the same Jean François
It two years before, the house had
uarters upstairs, while the offices for
ensive export-import business were
first floor. The unique railing is cast
sembling wrought iron. During the
the arched doorways were changed
granite pilasters, in style at the time.
hundred years later, the house was
d by General and Mrs. Kemper

Williams (who lived in the "Hidden House" behind, at 718 Toulouse). In 1966, their entire, very extensive collection of historic documents, paintings, books, photographs, etc., became The Historic New Orleans Collection. Their foundation preserves and adds to the material, making it available to the public in 10 galleries, a research library, tours and publications, all at 533 Royal.

The Spanish-Creole "Casa Comercio" at 534 Royal, has an arched "entresol," an arched carriage way and a wrought iron balcony. It was built soon after the fire of 1794, probably for businessmen Lille Sarpy and Juan Cortez.

*An "entresol" is the "half floor," hidden above the first floor, usually used for storage. Having no separate windows of its own, the "entresol" uses the top, "fan" section of the first story windows for its light, and appears from the outside, to be only a tall first story.*

During the 1920's and '30's, Lyle Saxon made this his home, while he wrote his wonderful books about New Orleans and her people. Saxon was responsible for encouraging many of his contemporaries to move into the Vieux Carré. His home was a haven for artists and writers and he helped many struggling creative people to develop their talents here.

Arriving from France just in time to help defeat the British in the Battle of New Orleans, François Seignouret planned to import high quality wines for the French Creoles of the Vieux Carré. In 1816, he built the handsome house at 520 Royal, with living quarters, a lovely patio and an "entresol" for the storage of the bottles. But, his fame grew, not from his wine, but from his skill at designing and making fine furniture. His treasured pieces can still be seen in some New Orleans homes and museums. Later, another respected wine merchant, Pierre Brutlatour rented the building.

*Left: Courtyard of the Seignouret House 520 Royal During the 1930's, The Arts and Crafts Club used the Seignouret House for its classes, exhibits and studios. They produced a wealth of wonderful artwork during the early 20th Century.*

Charles Dufau had two buildings erected at 501 Royal in 1806. Three years later, François Grandchamps rented the corner one to open a pharmacy. He did well and in 1821, was able to buy the building. One of his upstairs tenants was the noted American portrait painter, John Vanderlyn. Fashionable New Orleanians as well as plantation families came to sit for their portraits here.

The Royal Orleans Hotel stands at 500 Royal, in place of its predecessor, The St Louis Hotel, completed in 1838. The grand old hotel was the pride of the Vieux Carré (in competition with its "American Sector" counter part, the St. Charles Hotel). The Auction Exchange, under the hotel's huge dome, sold slaves, real estate and merchandise, and was very popular with planters and business men. There were fashionable balls held here nightly, and grand dinner

*...fore 1820, carriages along Royal Street either sent up clouds .. dust, or had wheels ..ired to their hubs in mud. When an experimental section ..f cobblestone paving did not disappear beneath the mud as ..redicted, a resolution was passed to pave Royal with stone. Because there is no local stone, ship ..aptains were offered 250 per ton to bring ..one, instead of sand ..rom Europe as ballast.*

parties. The large building was gutted by fire in 1841, but was immediately rebuilt. It was used for military and political headquarters during the Civil War and after, but financial problems caused the hotel to decline and gradually fall into disrepair.

Then for many years it stood empty, and in 1915, a fierce hurricane damaged its roof. It was torn down soon after, and the lot lay empty until 1960, when the present hotel was built (similar in size and character). Inside the lobby is a mural of the St. Louis Hotel in its prosperous heyday, done by New Orleans artist Boyd Cruise.

Antoine's Restaurant (a New Orleans landmark, at 713 St. Louis) has been owned and operated by five generations of the same family. It was begun by a young Frenchman, Antoine Alciatore, who had come to New Orleans from working in some of the great kitchens of France. He opened a small "pension," or café, on St. Louis, across from the newly opened St. Louis Hotel. It became popular for its good food and service. In 1868, he moved the restaurant into its present location. Eventually, the courtyard was closed in, other buildings connected, until today, the restaurant includes fourteen distinctive dining rooms. Memorabilia of Mardi Gras, family history and pictures of the many famous guests adorn the walls. Oysters Rockefeller were invented here, by Antoine's son Jules, and the restaurant is run today by the great, great grand children of the founder (with the next generation now in training).

At the corner of Conti and Royal stood Tortorici's Restaurant, run by the same family from 1900 until Katrina in 2005.

Among the many culinary innovations born in New Orleans is the "cocktail," invented by pharmacist, Antoine Peychaud. The buildings at 437 Royal (erected in 1800) housed a dry goods store on the corner and a pharmacy next door. Entertaining his fellow Masonic Lodge friends after hours, Peychaud prepared a mixture of brandy and his own special blend of bitters (Peychaud's is still sold today). Served in a double ended French egg cup (called a "coquetier") the drink took the name of the cup, and the English mispronunciation became cocktail.

In 1898, Hungarian immigrant William Feldman opened his Antique Emporium in this building, and, as with many merchants of the time, he and his family lived upstairs. Today, called Cohen and Sons, the fascinating store is operated by the fifth generation of William Feldman's family.

The elegant home at 427 Royal was built for Auguste Coudreau in 1859, when ornate cast iron galleries were the height of fashion. The Feldmans bought it in 1920 and furnished it with many of their beautiful antiques. Later, when the Great Depression hit, the Feldmans survived the hard times partially by charging five cents a person to tour the house and see their antiques.

An entire block of old Creole homes and businesses was torn down to build the imposing structure at 400 Royal, in 1908. First a courthouse, it was then home to the Department of Wildlife and Fisheries. It is surrounded by very old magnolia trees.

The unusual structure at 417 Royal was built in 1801 for Don José Faurie, a wealthy merchant, who bought the land from Vincent Rillieux (the great grandfather of painter Edgar Degas). Soon after, it was bought by the Banque de la Louisiane. (The monogram "LB" can be seen in the ironwork, and the iron plaque has two snakes, with two horns spilling coins – strange symbols for a bank to use !)

A wealthy Virginian, Martin Gordon, then bought the house. Prominent both socially and politically, the Gordons entertained many important visitors here, including Andrew Jackson in 1828. Later, when Gordon had financial difficulties, Judge Alonso Morphy acquired the home. His son Paul, at age 21, became Chess Champion of the World in 1858, when, in Paris, he played eight champion opponents simultaneously, with his back to the boards.

In 1955, the Brennan family moved their Bourbon Street restaurant into the old Casa Faurie, and added their name to New Orleans' great dining reputation. They are

most famous for their sumptuous and leisurely "Breakfast at Brennans." Their Creole specialties are served at tables both in and overlooking their lush courtyard.

The monogram in the rail of the 1807 house at 411 Royal, is that of the distinguished Dominique Rouquette, who raised his son Adrien here, to be a Creole gentleman. But, this young man listened to a different drummer. Having fallen in love with a Choctaw Indian girl who died, he decided to become a priest and open a mission among the Choctaws, living with them, adopting their dress and lifestyle. He was also known for his expressive poetry.

Jean Blanque was sent to New Orleans to be a French colonial official. He arrived in 1803, just as the French sold Louisiana to the United States. Living at 409 Royal, he soon distinguished himself in his new city, as a lawyer, merchant, banker and legislator. He also became the lawyer, friend and "business associate" of Jean Laffite, the brazen Barataria smuggler. He married Delphine Macarty, a gracious and charming hostess, whom we will meet later in the story of the "Haunted House."

The Old Louisiana State Bank, at 401 Royal, was designed by the architect Latrobe, one of the architects of the US capitol. He died of yellow fever in 1821, before this building was completed. The wrought iron balcony has the bank's initials. During the 1930's, it became the elegant antiques showroom of Bernard Manheim.

Don Pablo Lanusse, a senior judge in the Illustrious Cabildo, constructed the building at 343 Royal in 1800. Its wrought iron was crafted in Spain and is some of the finest in the Quarter. From 1811, the building was used as the Planters' Bank. Then, when the New Orleans Gas, Light and Banking Company took over, the French speaking population referred to it as the "Banque du Gaz," a name which the building retained long after the bank had closed. In 1880, Moise Waldhorn opened his antique shop here, continued by the next three generations of his family.

The handsome building at 334 Royal was constructed as the Bank of Louisiana in 1826, which closed for the Civil War. In 1871, the Royal Auction Exchange moved in and the building then became the City

Mortgage Office.    After World War I, it was home to the American Legion as well as a famous café, popular with the artists and writers of the 1920's and '30's. Later, the Tourist Commission and then the Police Department occupied the building.

Directly behind the Police Station lies a small street called Exchange Alley. It was built by the "New Orleans Improvement Company" in the 1830's, as an approach to the new St. Louis (Exchange) Hotel. The fourth block of the Alley was eliminated in the later construction of the Courthouse.

The block of Exchange, between Conti and Bienville was known for the many Fencing Masters who had their salons here. In the days when the slightest remark or gesture could be cause for an "affair d'honeur," young gentlemen came here for instruction in the use of the rapier. Many a tomb stone in the New Orleans cemeteries is inscribed, "Fell on the Field of Honor" (often in French). Though forbidden by both law and Church, dueling involved a code of honor and protocol that was a widely accepted method of settling men's differences. Even the governor, William Claiborne, fought the first duel under the American regime in 1803 !

*The corner of Rue Royale and Rue Conti was the financial center of the old Creole city for many years, with a bank on each of the corners. One of these was destroyed in the building of the huge Courthouse, but the other three still stand.*

*The corners where Royal Street meets Iberville and Bienville, each have large parking garages, which have been designed from the outside to closely resemble the old townhouses which once stood there.*

*Above: Brennan's Restaurant (The Old Casa Faurie) 417 Royal*

*Pepe Llulla, perhaps the most famous of all the fencing masters, had his popular "salle d'armes" in Exchange Alley. He had engaged in at least 20 duels and couldn't count how many times he had acted as a "second." In 1857, he purchased a cemetery, and many joked that it was to put his opponents in.*

*Below: The Old Louisiana State Bank, 401 Royal*

*Above: the Garde de Frise of a Royal Street balcony. "Garde de frise" is the French name for the ironwork, which decoratively protrudes at the end of a balcony (to prevent entry by climbing from another balcony or next door window).*

Prudent Mallard, who had learned his trade in his native France, came to New Orleans in the 1830's and opened a furniture shop at 301 Royal. Soon the furniture, designed and built in Mallard's Magasin, was as sought after by wealthy Creole planters and merchants, as that made by his competitor, François Seignouret. Mostly massive pieces, carved from exotic woods, Mallard furniture can be seen today in many museums and homes in New Orleans.

The Monteleone Hotel history is an American "Rags to Riches" story. Antonio Monteleone came from Sicily in 1880 and opened a cobbler's shop in the second block of Royal. Across the street was the 14 room, Commercial Hotel. Within five years, he had saved enough money to buy the hotel, and in 1893, he added 30 rooms and his own name to it. His son added a wing in 1928, with New Orleans' first hotel air conditioning. His grandson replaced the original section with another wing in 1956, and the hotel today is still in the capable hands of his descendants.

On Iberville, is a tall, galleried building at 725, built by the aristocratic François Gardère, as his mansion in 1832. Restaurant La Louisiane opened here in 1881. Under the direction of Ferdinand Alciatore (one of Antoine's many children) the restaurant became known for exceptional Creole cuisine. In the 1950's, it was owned by "Diamond Jim" Moran, who had been a shoeshine boy, prize fighter, bootlegger and body guard for Huey P. Long. He was known for wearing diamonds from head to foot (jewelry, belt buckle, shoestrings, glasses, etc). The restaurant later acquired the 1832 mansion next door, at 727 Iberville, to use for banquet rooms, and, during the 1960's, they rented it for several years to The New Orleans Playboy Club.

*Italians Ettore and Teresa Turci retired from the opera in 1917 and opened a respected Italian restaurant at 223 Bourbon. The couple would often sing to the customers and the restaurant was popular with visiting opera stars.*

*A glimpse through the iron gate of a carriage way or narrow side passage sometimes offers a stolen view of a quiet garden beyond.*

*Left: Gallatoires Restaurant,
209 Bourbon
Below: Arnaud's Restaurant,
813 Bienville*

*With a flair for the limelight, Germaine Cazenave Wells was queen of more Mardi Gras balls than any other woman in the city. Her regal costumes have been painstakingly preserved within Arnaud's in a Mardi Gras Museum. For years, she also rode in her own Easter Parade. Her version was a line of brightly decorated carriages bearing ladies in large Easter hats. They made their way through the Vieux Carré to the Cathedral, where they attended Easter Mass.*

Galatoire's, around the corner at 209 Bourbon, is one of the grand old Creole restaurants of the city, founded by French Jean Galatoire in 1905. His descendants still continue its fine traditions. The restaurant is famous for its extensive menu of Creole specialties, its distinctive original decor and its festive and unwavering customs. The 1831 building has unusual musical lyres in the balcony ironwork.

Arnaud's is another of the great French Creole restaurants that have contributed to the dining reputation, for which the city is justly famous. At 813 Bienville, Arnaud's was begun in 1918, by the grand mannered and congenial Frenchman, *Count* Arnaud Cazenave, For 30 years after his death, the popular restaurant was operated by his equally flamboyant daughter, Germaine. The succeeding proprietor - owner, though not of the same family, was inspired to restore the well known restaurant to its original decor, cuisine and fine reputation. The original main building dates from 1833, but the restaurant is made up of several adjoining old Creole

homes. The small one, on the corner of Bourbon and Bienville, was the Juncadella Grocery Store, built by the same Spaniards who constructed the Old Absinthe House, across the street, at 238 Bourbon.

Pedro Font and Francisco Juncadella (both from Spain) constructed that building for their importing business. It remained in their families for more than 100 years. In 1890, it became the Old Absinthe House, famous for its drink, the Absinthe Frappé.

Absinthe was a strong, licorice tasting liqueur, made from wormwood and herbs, which was outlawed in 1905, for causing

*It was during Prohibition, soon after revenue officers had raided and closed the Old Absinthe House (at 238 Bourbon) that a strange burglary took place. The thief broke into the closed bar and took paintings, the cash register and the old marble absinthe "drip fountain." Shortly after, these very same items appeared in a new "speak easy" in the 1838 building at 400 Bourbon. The same proprietor, Pierre Cazebonne, stood at the door. When Prohibition ended, there were two Old Absinthe Houses – the newer one being called thereafter, The Old Absinthe House Bar.*

*Left: "The Old Absinthe House," by George Pearce (238 Bourbon)*

*Above: The Olivier House, 828 Toulouse*

*Below: The Den of Mr. Hoy, 400 Dauphine.*

*"Bows and Arrows" decorate the iron railings at 327 Bourbon. The bows are of ribbon and tie the arrows together.*

brain damage. Now scientists have labeled absinthe a legal "spirit" and Absinthe drinks are once again made with the real thing.

Judah P. Benjamin was a Jewish lawyer, statesman and U.S. Senator who lived in the house of his father-in-law at 327 Bourbon. Born in the West Indies, Benjamin had entered Yale Law School at age 14. During the Civil War, as Attorney General for the South, he was often called "the brains of the Confederacy." At War's end, he fled to exile in England. Studying again, he became prominent at the *English* Bar. His wife's father, Aguste St. Martin, a well to do planter, built this town house (with its unusual mansard roof) in 1835.

The Royal Sonesta Hotel stands at Bourbon and Bienville. The hotel's courtyard has a removable canvas "roof," to protect the tropical plants during the few "below freezing" days of the New Orleans winters. On the second floor, several of John James Audubon's prints, from his *Birds of America*, are displayed.

Theophilus Hyde was a prosperous wholesale grocer, who built the grand home

at 840 Conti, soon after his wife Agalia Conrotte inherited the land from her father in 1828. One of its architects, George Clarkson, was killed in a duel before the building was completed.

The typical home at 400 Dauphine fit well into this nice neighborhood when it was built in 1836. But in 1885, newspapers were complaining about the "notorious Opium den" in the building, run by a Chinese man named Mr. Hoy.

Edouard Bertus, one of the best dancing masters in the city, had the home at 826 St. Louis built for him in 1842, while he was living in the house next door at 832. It was sold five years later to Elizabeth Belin, widow of Louis Levant. Since levant means rising in French, some contend that this was "Le Sol Levant" or "The House of the Rising Sun" – the famous bordello. Others insist that this house has always been occupied by prominent and "respectable" families. There are several buildings that could be the House of the Rising Sun.

Hermann Grima House, at 820 St. Louis, is a restored 1831 house that is open to the public for informative and interesting touring. Built for Samuel Hermann, a wealthy merchant, the house sold in 1844 to Judge Felix Grima, whose family lived here for five generations. In 1924, the house

*"Dixie," the nickname for the South, originated in New Orleans. During the city's Golden Age, The Citizen's Bank of Louisiana, issued its bank notes in both French and English. The French word for ten is "Dix," and northern river boat men would say they were going south to the land of "Dixies" The name stuck, first in the city and then in the entire South.*

*Street vendors were a common sight in the Vieux Carré, even into the 1950's. Men carried clothes poles, tin goods, palmetto fronds (for cleaning out chimneys) or sun dried Spanish Moss (for mattress stuffing). There were also familiar horse or mule drawn wagons, like the Kerosene Cart, and the Oyster Wagon.*

became a haven for women in need, operated by the Christian Women's Exchange. They supported their work, for many years, with the proceeds from "The Courtyard Kitchen," which served "Tea and Luncheon" in the garden. Today, they offer an authentic look into the life of Creole households in the "Golden Era" before the Civil War. The paintings and furnishings from wealthy Creole homes of the time include many pieces from the original families. The actual kitchen, stables and courtyard can also be viewed.

Around the corner at 505 Dauphine is a cottage where the naturalist-painter John James Audubon stayed in 1821-1822 while working on his monumental series *Birds of America*. (He painted 167 of his 435 different birds in Louisiana, between 1821 and 1830). While living at this address, Audubon earned his living painting portraits of prominent Creoles and their families. He also spent many hours in the French Market, studying the game birds brought in for sale there.

The grand home at 521 Dauphine was built by Spaniard Angel Xiques, who had made his fortune importing cigars, coffee and other products from Cuba. He had the famous architect Du Pouilly design the imposing home in 1851. After his death in

1867, the house changed hands and later became a disreputable "palace of chance," run by Cuban Emanuel Rodriguez.

Marianne Bienvenue was only sixteen, when she married Nicholas Olivier, a very wealthy planter and already a widower with a large family. He died a few years later, leaving his young bride to raise his twelve children. When she began construction of the elegant home at 828 Toulouse, in 1836, she already had fifty living grandchildren. Madame Olivier's mansion was beautifully furnished and decorated with *objects d'art* which she imported from Paris. The courtyard, the 14 - 16 foot ceilings, the carriageway and winding staircase of this restored mansion (now a hotel) can still be seen.

In an inexpensive room at 516 Bourbon, the writer, Lafcadio Hearn, labored over his wonderful stories. Having arrived penniless in 1877, he was a well known figure in the French Quarter for ten years. His tales were written in English, but set in the exotic, French speaking Vieux Carré. Half blind and always poor, his writing was mostly for newspapers, expressing his fascination for

*Above: The original kitchen of the Herman Grima House, 820 St. Louis*

*New Orleans has businesses, which specialize in the salvage and selling of old hardware, fixtures and architectural pieces from old homes and stores.*

the culture, customs, architecture and mélange of speech of his adopted city.

The Old French Opera House stood at 541 Bourbon. When the grand building was erected in 1859, New Orleans already had a great love for music, drama and opera. The five levels of the ornately decorated hall were packed nightly during many seasons. Most of the Mardi Gras balls (and other fashionable balls) were held here as well. The buildings in the blocks near the French Opera House all housed shops which catered to the opera productions or the balls—wig makers, tailors, mask makers, etc. The street is still indented here, where the carriages stopped to let off their elegant passengers.

Opera productions in the Vieux Carré were mostly in French and the Creoles knew the operas by heart. The "Negro Gallery" on the fourth tier was always full, and the laborers on the wharves whistled the arias as accurately as the "ladies and gentlemen," who sang them in their parlors. Arguments, and even duels, were fought over the merits of favorite stars.

When the French Opera House burned down in 1919, Lyle Saxon wrote in the morning paper, "the heart of the old French Quarter stopped beating last night." Though deeply missed by all, it was never rebuilt and the lot stood empty until the 1960's, when a modern hotel was built.

The cottage at 600 Bourbon was constructed before 1800, probably for Amedée Langevine, while across the street, 601 dates from 1777. Even with such small cottages, the slave quarters were substantial in proportion.

The old house at 611 Bourbon was built by Jacques Lebrun in 1808. Constructed in 1812, 619 still shows the remains of its original red tile roof, once so common in the Vieux Carré. Its owner, Arsene Latour designed the defensive "earthworks" for the Battle of New Orleans. The corner house, at 614, was built before1810, by Jean Soulié.

The well respected notary, Don Esteban de Quiñones, built himself a grand home at 623 Bourbon in 1795. The house has fine ironwork, both wrought and cast, a fan window and carriageway. In recent years, Congresswoman Lindy Boggs, another well respected public figure, made it her home.

The tall home at 624 Bourbon has retained its wrought iron balconies. It was built by Émile Peron in 1800, soon after his arrival from Santo Domingo.

*Left: The LePrêtre House*
*716 Dauphine (story on following page)*
*Right: Glimpse of the huge courtyard of*
*the Court of Two Sisters, 615 Royal*

*Above: The Cornstalk Fence, 915 Royal*

The Bourbon House was a restaurant - bar at 700 Bourbon, during the 1940's and '50's, popular with the Bohemian literary and artistic community. A Jazz Funeral was held for it, when it closed in the 1960's.

Built for dentist Joseph Gardette in 1836, the dramatic house at 716 Dauphine was owned by the family of wealthy planter Jean Baptiste Le Prêtre for almost 50 years. A legend tells that a Sultan's brother later rented the house, after absconding with several members of the Sultan's harem, his jewels, and the ship and crew that brought them to New Orleans. The brother entertained lavishly, generating much gossip about the royal ladies who lived with him. Then one morning, he and his harem were all found stabbed to death – the ship and crew missing from their River moorings. Had the Sultan sent the assassins? Had the ship's crew done it? Some said that they stole the jewels and fled to become pirates!

At the end of Orleans, just outside the Ramparts (the wall that surrounded the original city – leaving the name Rampart Street) was Congo Square, an area where slaves were allowed to gather on Sunday afternoons for dancing. (The French and Spanish forbid any slave assembly, for fear of rebellion, but the Americans saw it as a safety valve to prevent rebellion.) As many as 2,000 people gathered (dancers, vendors, spectators, patrolling soldiers, hustlers, and "side shows"). Accompanied by home made instruments, the dancers grew more sensual and frenzied as the pulse of the drums grew faster. A cannon, fired in the Place d'Armes, was the curfew for all slaves to return home. The site of Congo Square is now Louis Armstrong Park.

John Davis built a large hall at 717 Orleans, to hold nightly balls for white "society." In 1838, these "society" balls moved to the St. Louis Hotel, and his Salle d'Orleans became the home of the very different "Quadroon Balls." (Quadroon meant one fourth Negro - usually a white father and Mulatto mother). Mothers would bring their beautiful Quadroon daughters to dance with white gentlemen of means, chaperoning the girls closely. A match would result in an "arrangement," the man to provide for the girl in a cottage nearby. Some of these liaisons were broken, upon the man's marriage to a white wife. (A "settlement" would be made, giving the woman the cottage and provision for herself and their children.) But many bonds continued for life, the man supporting and educating two families at once. Though practiced for many years, resulting in many tears, duels and suicides, the entire system was something that was never discussed or acknowledged in front of white women.

The Civil War ended the Quadroon Balls. In 1881, the Davis hall became part of a convent for an order of Black Nuns. Now part of a hotel, the old ballroom can still be viewed.

Count Louis Philippe Joseph de Roffignac fled the guillotine in France and came to New Orleans. He became a successful merchant, fought in the Battle of New Orleans and was elected Mayor. His terms of office were years of needed civic improvements. His wealthy father-in-law, Dr. Joseph Montague, had built the house at 731 Royal before 1799, and gave the adjoining lot to his daughter and Roffignac to build their home at 721 Royal.

The Irishman, Daniel Clark, adopted Creole New Orleans and became one of its most prominent citizens. He built his home at 823 Royal and was the area's first representative to Congress in 1803. He wounded Gov. Claiborne in a duel. As a successful merchant, he was both an agent of Jean Lafitte and a friend of the future King of France, Louis Philippe. He became the richest man in Louisiana in the early 1800's. After his death, Myra Clark Gaines claimed to be his daughter and only heir, creating a legal case that lasted for 50 years.

On December 23, 1814, a large group of prominent ladies gathered in the home of Madame Porée, at 840 Royal, to await together the outcome of the first skirmish with the British. Terrified, they huddled together in prayer. At last, in the darkness, came the hoof beats of a rider. Crowding onto the balcony, they heard a young Creole shout, "Victory" – the British had been defeated – the city was saved - so far!

The three attached brick Miltenberger Mansions at 902 Royal, were constructed in 1838 by the widowed Marie Miltenberger for her three sons. Each of the houses was changed over the years, as the brothers raised their families there. In 1858, with a Miltenberger in the cast iron business, the original wrought iron rails were replaced with the more ornate cast ones.

The unusual little "parapet double," at 707 Dumaine, is the only survivor of its once common style in this block. The high parapet of Spanish tile allowed the family to sit out on the roof in the evenings (instead of the balcony of a larger building). It was built in 1800 for a Spanish soldier, Don Joachim de la Torré.

The picturesque cottage, at 941 Bourbon, is Laffite's Blacksmith Shop, built in 1772, in the old French, "brick between post" style. The blacksmith business of Jean Laffite and his brothers, served as a "front" for their illegal smuggling trade. In 1807, the importation of slaves into the US was

*Left: Gen. Labatut's House, 623 Royal (story on page 21)*

*The large and sturdy building at 701 Bourbon was constructed for Jean Balthazar Georges in 1811, and is fastened together with wooden pegs*

*Left: Lafitte's Blacksmith Shop, a brick-between-post cottage, 941 Bourbon. "Brick between post" was the construction style used in much of the early architecture of the Vieux Carré, most of which was lost in the Great Fire of 1788. The soft, locally made brick and mortar had little strength, and were used to fill in the spaces between large upright and diagonal posts, which gave the buildings their strength. The walls were then covered with stucco to protect the materials from the elements. The later, taller buildings were usually made from a much stronger brick, imported from the Northeast.*

*Left: The Miltenberger Mansions, 902 Royal*

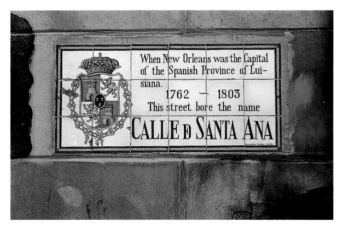

outlawed, but slavery itself was still legal – the perfect conditions to encourage smuggling. The Laffites did a thriving business in capturing slaves from foreign ships and smuggling them to buyers (including the Church!). In the maze of waterways south of the city, the privateers and smugglers, known as the Baratarians, had their commune headquarters.

McDonogh 15 Public School is the large red brick building on the 700 block of St. Philip. It is one of 35 public schools, built with money endowed by John McDonogh to the children of New Orleans in 1850. McDonogh had become very rich during the early 1800's from several businesses and a large plantation. But his "strange" ideas were regarded with suspicion, despite his prominence. (He crossed the Mississippi by rowboat to save the ferry fare! He believed in educating slaves! He provided schooling and "work for wages" to the slaves on his plantation, preparing them to buy their freedom !) He was regarded as an eccentric old miser. But happily, upon his death, he had bequeathed the money to establish a public school system for the city. Many of his original schools are still in use.

The "Great Creole," General P.G.T.

Beauregard, Southern hero of the Civil War, lived in the house at 934 Royal with his son, René, after his return from the war. Many in New Orleans believed that the outcome of the war might have been different if he had been given a position of leadership. Unusual iron lovebirds adorn the gate.

After the Battle of New Orleans in 1815, when the "danger" had passed, General Andrew Jackson did not lift the Martial law. This displeased many of the civilian soldiers, who wished to return to "normal" life. When a judge ruled against Jackson, the General had the judge arrested. Later, in the building at 919 Royal (then used as a courthouse) Jackson was fined $1,000 for contempt of court. A crowd at Maspero's Exchange raised money for his fine, but he donated it to the widows and children of those killed in defense of the city.

The famous "Cornstalk Fence" guards the house at 915 Royal. Its cast morning glories and cornstalks were shipped from Philadelphia in about 1850 to Dr. Joseph Biamenti, as a gift to his wife, who missed the rural scenery of the Midwest. The fence survived, when the original house burned.

Gallier House, at 1132 Royal, is the home that famous New Orleans architect

James Gallier, Jr. built for himself in 1857. He was the designer of the French Opera House and his father had designed the City Hall and many Garden District homes. This house remained in the family until 1917. It was later restored and is now a museum, which offers an authentic look into New Orleans life of the 1860's.

The strange building at 1140 Royal has been known for years as the "Haunted House." When Madame Delphine Macarty LaLaurie married her third husband, they moved into this newly completed mansion in 1832. Soon it was the scene of many elegant parties. Madame LaLaurie, from the finest of Creole families, was known as a gracious and harming hostess. But.....there was gossip about her slaves – the young slave girl who had fallen to her death in the courtyard - the authorities had found no wrongdoing.......Then in 1834, there was a fire in the house. When helpful neighbors rushed in to put it out and save the lavish furnishings, they discovered a secret room, with seven slaves, chained, starved and tortured. When word spread, a mob gathered outside, waiting for Madame to appear. Instead, a carriage suddenly burst from the gates and the LaLauries fled,

eventually to France. The house is said to be haunted by the sad souls of her slaves.

The row of houses at 1105-1141 Royal was known as Architects' Row, built by an architectural firm on speculation in 1832. Originally identical, there have been many changes made. The two closest to Gov. Nicholls Street are the most original.

Around the corner at 716 Gov. Nicholls, Judge Gallien Preval built public stables in 1834 to be used by the families living in Architects' Row. Later, second stories were added, to make the buildings apartments.

John Gauché was a very successful merchant and importer of crockery and china. He constructed the grand "villa" at 704 Esplanade for himself in 1856, importing the ornate cast iron from Germany.

Attorney Henry Raphael Denis had three adjoining homes built in 1834, at 602-626 Esplanade. Keeping the corner one, he sold 604 to Judge Alonzo Morphy and 606 to Judge Felix Grima.

The mansion at 544 Esplanade was built as a "double" house in 1860, with two front doors and no iron trim or railings. In 1920, "Count" Arnaud Cazenave (of Arnaud's Restaurant) bought the left side of the building, but had to wait 11 years to acquire

*Above: The Beauregard-Keyes House, 1113 Chartres*

*The "Casket Girls" were sent to the colony in response to Bienville's pleas for wives for his settlers. Unlike the first shiploads of criminals from French jails, these girls were from "proper" families and put in the care of the Nuns, until their marriages could be arranged. In New Orleans, it has always been prestigious to trace one's ancestry back to a casket girl.*

the other half. Remodeling, he removed the center wall, made one grand doorway and added the iron railings and decor.

While Andrew Jackson was President in 1835, Congress approved construction of the New Orleans Mint, at 400 Esplanade. It produced coins from 1837 until 1910. It became part of the Louisiana State Museum and contains some wonderful displays of Mardi Gras and Jazz history. In 1862, distraught Southerner William Mumford, tore down the US flag in front of the Mint. He was hanged there, for his "crime."

The Old Ursuline Convent stands at 1112 Chartres. This French stuccoed-brick building may be the oldest structure in the Mississippi Valley. The Ursuline Nuns arrived at the little colony in 1727, beginning the first schools and orphanages, (as well as caring for the "casket girls"). This large, *new* convent was built for them in 1749, to replace their old quarters here. They moved from this building in 1824.

The author, Frances Parkinson Keyes, bought the Greek Revival house at 1113

Chartres in 1944, saving it from demolition. An auctioneer, Joseph LeCarpentier, had built it in 1826. The house is open to the public and honors the "Great Creole," Gen. P.G.T. Beauregard, leader in the 1840's War with Mexico, engineer of several US forts, Commandant of West Point and decorated Confederate General.

Joseph Guillot built the house at 623 Ursuline in 1825, while the unusual building at 627 was constructed in 1838 by Monsieur O. Duplantier. Across the street, at 620, the distinguished Nicolas de LaLande built his home. While living here in 1818, LaLande was murdered on his doorstep by a pirate.

Joseph Marie Fernandez built the stately home at 616 Ursuline in 1832. It is one of the locations rumored to have later been the House of the Rising Sun. The 1807 townhouse at 1021 Chartres was the home of Major General Pierre Denis Delaronde, important in the Battle of New Orleans.

Madame John's Legacy is the name that was given to the house at 632 Dumaine. The raised French colonial building is

*Above: The "Fire Mark" House (a typical small cottage double) 613 Dumaine (story, page 42)*

*During the Great Depression, William Warrington had a charity school in the 1825 house, at 623 Ursuline. He used several other houses in this neighborhood, as trade schools and shelters.*

*Right: The Formento House, 823 Chartres (story, page 42)*

*Left: Madame John's Legacy, painting by James Kendrick, III The building, (632 Dumaine) is one of the two oldest structures in the Mississippi Valley. The name, "Madame John's Legacy" comes from a story by George W. Cable, about a Quadroon woman named Zalli, who was left the house by a dying bachelor named John.*

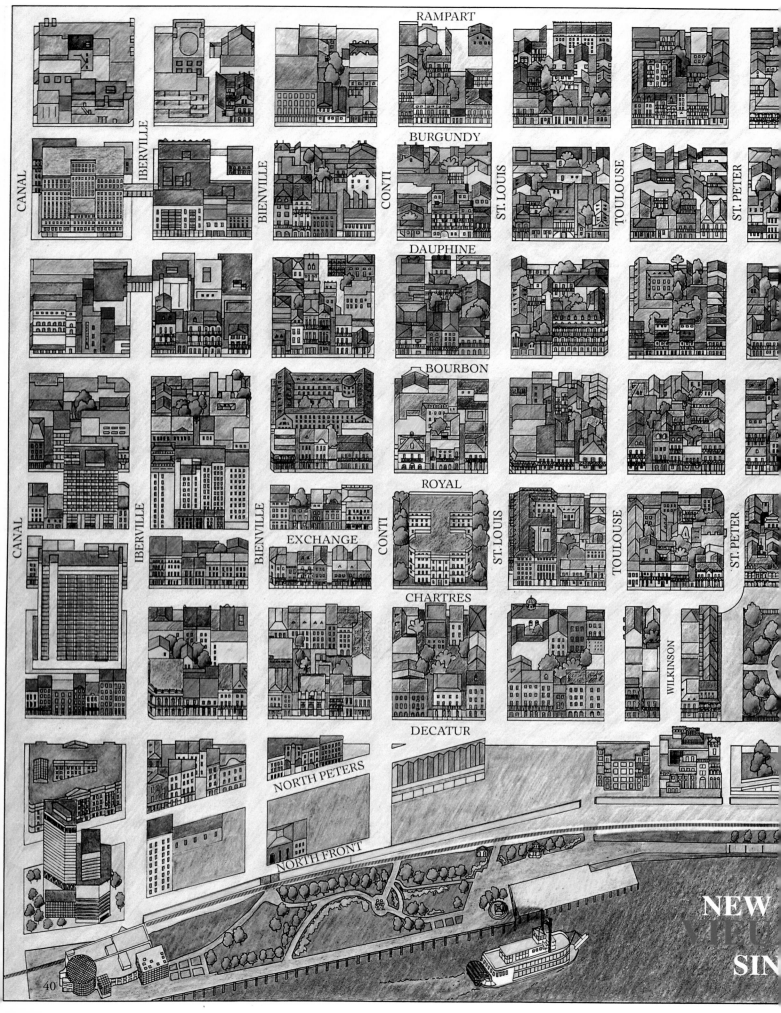

RAMPART

CANAL

IBERVILLE

BIENVILLE

BURGUNDY

CONTI

DAUPHINE

ST. LOUIS

TOULOUSE

ST. PETER

CANAL

IBERVILLE

BIENVILLE

EXCHANGE

CONTI

BOURBON

ROYAL

ST. LOUIS

TOULOUSE

ST. PETER

WILKINSON

CHARTRES

DECATUR

NORTH PETERS

NORTH FRONT

NEW

SIN

RAMPART

BURGUNDY

DAUPHINE

BOURBON

ROYAL

CHARTRES

DECATUR

ST. ANN

DUMAINE

ST. PHILIP

URSULINE

GOV. NICHOLS

BARRACKS

ESPLANADE

PERE ANTOINE

MADISON

FRENCH MARKET PLACE

NORTH PETERS

LEANS

1718

*Below: Raw oysters
have been a treat in
New Orleans, from
the earliest years*

typical of the larger homes in the Vieux Carré, before the 1788 fire. One of the two oldest structures in the Mississippi Valley, it was built in 1726, by sea captain Jean Pascal. The controversy over its age centers on whether it was rebuilt, or simply repaired, after the fire. During the 1770's, René Beluche lived here. He was an important captian among the Barataria smugglers.

Across the street is a little house, at 613, with a small metal plaque on its front, called a fire mark, (photo, page 38). During the 1800's, fire insurance companies, put "marks" on the houses of their policy holders, to direct their own volunteer fire fighters to the buildings which they insured. In 1891, when a paid, municipal fire department was finally established, the era of using fire marks came to an end.

The house at 823 Chartres, a favorite with artists, was built by Dr. Felix Formento in 1835 (photo, page 38).

The corner structure, at 801Chartres, was built

as a home above a store, in 1902. It was converted in 1924, to be the Taormina Macaroni Factory, during the years when the French Quarter was home to thousands of newly arrived Italians.

Marcus Tio, a wealthy merchant and slave trader, had to rebuild his home at 625 St. Ann, after it burned in the Great Fire of 1788.

Directly behind the Cabildo on St. Peter, is The Armory, built in 1839, on the site of the old Spanish prison, known as the Calabozo or Calaboose. The new building was also home to the Louisiana Legion, a prestigious military organization for officers from the "best" families.

Mayor John Watkins lived in the house at 630 St. Peter in 1806. It had been built a few years before by the Merciers, a family of doctors and writers. In 1923, it became the home of Countess Irma Von Einsiedel and her large collection of antiques.

The unusual building at 620 St. Peter was erected for Victor David in 1838. In 1925, Le Petit Salon was founded here, dedicated to the preservation of culture, traditions and the historic atmosphere of the Vieux Carré. Made up mostly of prominent literary women, it was first headed by New Orleans author, Grace King.

On the corner at 600 St. Peter, a Spanish tavern being built, was disrupted by the two great fires and finally completed in 1796.

*Right: The
wrought iron
gate of old
Preservation
Hall, 726
St. Peter*

The Drawing Room Players was a theater group formed in 1916. They were so successful, that in 1922, they rebuilt this old tavern and added an "old looking" building behind it to be their permanent theater. The hall seats 500 people and hosts a full calendar of productions annually.

When the well to do merchant Bartholome Bosqué built his home at 617 Chartres, it had a flat Spanish roof and the doorways were arched. He had his initials "BB" put into the wrought iron railing. The house was changed, later, to be more "modern."

In 1796, Joseph Reynes traded a tract of plantation land and a slave for the property at 601 Chartres. He built his mansion here, and then sold it in 1830 for $20,000.

The home at 628 Toulouse, was built by François Jacob in 1813, as his townhouse. The fan windows and picturesque court yard have always been popular with artists.

The unusual structure at 541 Chartres was built to house the ice making equipment of the Cosmopolitan Ice Company in 1907. The style of roof (flat, with pots of yucca or cactus on it) was typical of much older, Spanish buildings, like the Cabildo and the Bosqué House (which were each later given pitched roofs).

The Great Fire of 1788 began in the large house at 538 Chartres. Don Vincente Nuñez was paymaster of the Spanish army when he had the three adjoining town houses built in 1783. Five years later, his Good Friday candles, burning before a shrine in his corner, second floor home, set the curtains ablaze. The fire burned 856 buildings in just four hours. Ironically, the strong wind which spread the flames so quickly, kept them from destroying his house. Badly damaged, it was bought in 1794, by Louis Galley.

In 1817, the piece of land at 508 Toulouse was included on a list of property to be auctioned at Maspero's Exchange. The buyer constructed a Creole building to house his business below, storage in the entresol and living quarters above. In recent years, the building had steel rods inserted through

43

*Above: Dufilho's Pharmacie Museum, 514 Chartres*

*Below: Displays from Dufilho's actual apothecary shop, open from the 1820's to 1855, in this building.*

the floors to take the load off the aging timbers and brick. The ends of the bolts are visible on the outer right wall.

In 1816, Louis Dufilho had become the first licensed pharmacist in America. Seven years later, he built his new *Pharmacie* at 514 Chartres and moved his family upstairs. He had a botanical garden in the courtyard to supply medicinal herbs. In 1950, his old *Pharmacie* became a museum, which shows interesting displays from the 1800's, including medical and pharmaceutical tools, cosmetics, voodoo potions and an 1855 Italian marble soda fountain.

When the French Creole population of New Orleans learned of Napoleon's escape from Elba in 1815, they were wild with enthusiasm. Perhaps Bonaparte would consider taking refuge in *their* French city ! Mayor Girod offered his home, at 500 Chartres, to be the "Royal Quarters."

When it was learned that Napoleon was exiled on St. Helena, the Mayor was part of a plot to rescue their hero and bring him to New Orleans. A racing schooner, *The Seraphine,* to be under the command of the smuggler Dominique You, was outfitted for the ocean trip, when the news arrived of the Emperor's death. The Napoleon House, (as the mayor's home became known) was built before 1798, as a two story house. It was acquired by Girod in 1814. The third floor

*Catherine Macnamara, wife of Judge Merieult (533 Royal) had a head of golden hair – unusual in a city of dark haired beauties. The story goes, that Napoleon was trying to secure a treaty with the Sultan of Turkey, who was trying to buy a blonde wig for one of his harem. When the Merieults were on business in Europe, Napoleon offered Madame increasing amounts of gold, if she would sell her hair. She steadfastly refused, and returned to New Orleans, hair intact.*

*"Double" is the local term for houses, built together as "twins", which share a common center wall.*

*A "Shotgun House" refers to the common style of New Orleans house, with the main rooms in a line, behind one another, and no hallway. (A shot fired through the front door could pass through all the rooms without hitting anything.)*

and cupola were added later. The restaurant - bar, which bears the same name, is very unusual. Its old walls are decorated with sketches and paintings of Napoleon.

Across the street is a remnant of wall from the old St. Louis Hotel, incorporated in the modern hotel. In 1915, the city launched a massive project to rid itself of rats (and the Plague they periodically spread). The empty hotel was torn down, in the energetic fervor that destroyed over two million rats and their nesting sites.

The wealthy Creole planter, Jean Noel d'Estrehan, built the townhouse at 400 Chartres in 1802. In 1825, his widow sold it to François Marie Perrilliar, who had his initials put into the wrought iron balcony.

The year of the Great Fire, Don Juan Paillet bought the charred ruins of Don Narcisco Alva's house at 440 Chartres and built the stuccoed-brick building which stands today. His tenant, Pierre Maspero, opened a very popular coffee house and auction exchange. Planters, politicians, judges, newspaper men, soldiers and merchants gathered to discuss politics, prices and crops, to hear the official news

of the day and to attend the auctions. It was here that a citizens' meeting in 1814, created the Committee of Public Safety to organize a defense for the city against the British, while awaiting the arrival of General Jackson. Some say that it was in the entresol of Maspero's, that Jackson had his secret meeting with Jean Laffite to plan the strategy for the city's defense.

*Above: The Napoleon House, 500 Chartres*

*Below: Maspero's Auction Exchange, 440 Chartres*

*Above: In the Farmer's Market, 1100 N. Peters (part of the Old French Market)*

*Below: "The Fruit Peddler," detail from an historic, period painting by Boyd Cruise, courtesy The Historic New Orleans Collection*

On Decatur, near Jackson Square, stands the large structure that was built in 1891, as the Jackson Brewing Company (which produced Jax Beer). An important local industry, it closed in 1974. The building was converted into a riverfront dining and shopping center in 1983.

At 800 Decatur is the oldest "coffee stand" still in the Vieux Carré, the Café du Monde. Café au lait and beignets have been a tradition here since the 1860's and are available any time of day or night.

The Old French Market, which stands along the next blocks of Decatur, actually began more as an Indian market, when Choctaw women spread their mats along the river bank with herbs and baskets for sale. They were soon joined by German farmers, selling garden and dairy products from their nearby farms. The Spanish erected an official market building in 1791, which was replaced with the new, arcaded structure for the butchers in 1813. The Bazaar was built in the next block in 1822, and the Vegetable Market in 1872. These substantial buildings all underwent re-modeling in the 1930's, with the WPA, and again in the 1970's, by the City.

The Market was always crowded, noisy and fragrant. Strong odors mingled and contrasted – sweet smells of freshly baked goods, molasses and fruits, steaming coffee, herbs and garlic, live chickens, cheeses, meats, fish, oysters and crabs, as well as the delivery wagon mules, crowded nearby. A rich babble of many languages included vendors calling out their specials and women bartering prices. The sounds of chickens and birds were occasionally drowned out by a steamboat, an organ grinder or a brass band. Novelties, such as parrots, monkeys or alligators in cages, con men selling "cure alls" and street entertainers were common. Sundays in the Market were especially festive and the Sunday commerce and gaiety shocked the Puritan Americans, who discouraged any work or festivities on the Sabbath.

*"Beignets," pronounced Ben-yays, are hot French "doughnuts," sprinkled with powdered sugar - usually accompanied by "Café au Lait," strong, dark roast coffee with chicory, poured equally with steaming milk.*

*Chicory is the roasted root of the endive plant, often used to flavor coffee in New Orleans.*

*"Lagniappe," pronounced Lan-yap, was the "little something extra," which a merchant would give his customer*

The Farmers' Market at 1100 N. Peters is the nation's oldest operating produce market, selling vegetables, fruits, spices and seafood. The last building of the Market serves as a Flea Market, renting space to vendors selling a variety of goods, from the unique, collectable or hand made, to common "dime store" bargains

Across from the Market, at 823 Decatur, Hippolyte Begué and his wife, Madame Begué, began serving a leisurely second breakfast (with many courses and wine) to the butchers and produce men of the market, during the 1850's.

Along Decatur, many Italian families opened their grocery stores, during the late 1800's and early 1900's, catering to the workmen of the market and riverfront. Large, freshly made sandwiches, such as muffaletas and po'boys, became popular items in these stores, and remain so today.

Gallatin Street was the name of the street which ran along the Market, from Ursuline to Barracks St. During the mid 1800's, it was one of the most dangerous parts of the city. Prostitutes and criminals preyed on the bar and dance hall customers. Many unwary young men were mugged, murdered or shanghaied, if they ventured there. Later, many of the buildings were torn down to build the Farmers' Market, and the remaining old structures now house

produce or interesting shops and cafés.

The Hotel de la Marine at 923 Decatur, and the Café des Refugees, next door, were favorite meeting and drinking spots of the Baratarian smugglers and prominent French men, exiled by the Revolution in France or the uprising in Santo Domingo. Historian Lyle Saxon describes a birthday dinner, held here for one of Napoleon's ex-generals, attended by smugglers, pirates, financiers, merchants and attorneys.

The Riverfront Streetcar runs along the riverfront, from the French Market all the way to the New Orleans Convention Center in the Central Business District.

Reconstruction of the river levees was a continuous process, from the earliest days of the colony, in an effort to control the flooding of the Mississippi. The modern levee makes the banks of the river very high, so that at times of high water, ships pass by, so high above the level of the streets, that it creates an eerie effect.

The Moon Walk, across from Jackson Square, offers a wonderful view of the River, up close. The Mississippi River Bridge opened in 1958 - its twin span added in 1984. The free Ferry Boats can be seen, as they continually cross from one bank to the other. Here, on this shore, is where it all began, where Bienville first envisioned his capital city, La Nouvelle Orleans.

*Above: "St. Louis at Royal" by James Kendrick, III, New Orleans painter*

*Above Center: The Steamboat wharves, during the Golden Age - barrels of molasses and sugar, bales of cotton - stevedores, sailors, merchants, inspectors, passengers, vendors and soldiers – all the commerce and travel of the whole Mississippi Valley, to and from the rest of the world. It all came through New Orleans - steamboats and ships, as far as one could see !*

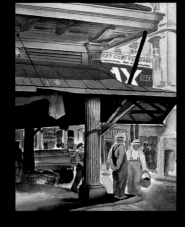

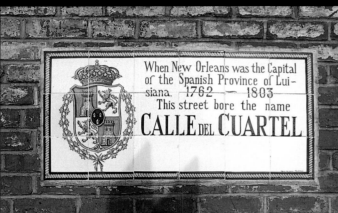

When New Orleans was the Capital of the Spanish Province of Lui-siana. 1762 — 1803 This street bore the name CALLE DEL CUARTEL

*B*oyd Cruise came to New Orleans in 1928, to study art at the Arts and Craft Club (in the Seignouret House). Later, after studying in Philadelphia and Europe, he returned to New Orleans in 1935 to live. These watercolors of New Orleans buildings, were part of both a W.P.A. project and an Historic American Buildings Survey.

The intertwining of history and art is a combination which he continued though out his life. His fine "historic" paintings (some shown in this book) have given us "windows into the past," with his careful study and recording of every detail of architecture, lifestyle and people of the city, in earlier times.

He worked with the Vieux Carré Commission and other organizations to save and preserve historic buildings, as well as to promote artistic, cultural and historic endeavors in New Orleans. For many years, his time was devoted to The Historic New Orleans Collection, in collecting, organizing, researching and preserving art, information and historical materials for New Orleans.

*Early "contemporary" watercolors of the Vieux Carré, by Boyd Cruise, courtesy, The Louisiana State Museum*

# VOODOO

V oodoo was introduced in New Orleans by slaves, brought in from the West Indies. Most of the people who were captured in Africa by slavers, were transported to the Caribbean Islands, as a sort of "holding station," while they were assessed and "trained" (for jobs of servitude). They were also "taught" Christianity. Under the British, Africans were instructed in Protestant Christianity, while the French and Spanish taught them Catholicism. In the French Islands, slaves blended their religious beliefs and rituals from Africa, with those of Catholicism, forming a powerful new religion called Voodoo. Most New Orleans slaves came from these French Islands and brought their Voodoo with them.

In the beginning, Voodoo was regarded as being against the beliefs of the Church. And, since *any* gathering of slaves was considered dangerous, authorities forbid the practice. But, the Voodoo beliefs and rituals continued in secret, flourishing in the unique culture of the city.

During the 1800's, Voodoo was transformed into a distinctly New Orleans version of the cult, largely due to the influence of the most famous Voodoo Queen, Marie Laveau. Born in 1794, a free Mulatto, she grew up in the Vieux Carré. Becoming a hairdresser, she had intimate conversations with upper class women, giving her both the closeness and method for gaining personal information and confidences, that she could later use.

She had practiced Voodoo for many years, when she decided to take over from the "reigning" Voodoo queens of the city. Not only did she become the undisputed Queen, but she changed the very purpose of the beliefs, to make herself a good profit. Realizing that people were hungry for answers to their prayers and desires, she offered them solutions, with so much cleverness and showmanship, that her Voodoo powers soon became famous, and she was respected, feared and well paid.

She always did her own secret research into each problem, so that she could manipulate the outcome, with the appearance of "magical" powers. She had a huge serpent - Zombi - that lived in a large Alabaster box. Most people believed that Zombi ate small children, when allowed, and that all kinds of evil was possible from bad spirits. They thought themselves dependent on the Queen's connections with the spirit world, to protect them.

The main tool of a Voodoo was the "gris-gris" (pronounced gree gree). The classic form, familiar to most, is the small cloth doll, into which one sticks pins to cause an effect. But a gris-gris could also be

in the form of a small bag of powder or particular combinations of hair, feathers, bones, leaves or pebbles, usually tied with a "special" string or sprinkled with salt, ashes or herbs. Placing the gris-gris on the designated doorstep, or pillow, had the power to change the future for the "client" – a lover assured, a rival defeated, an election won or a financial triumph. A rabbit's foot, cat's tail or other lucky charm, might be given to the "client" to wear. It took a good Voodoo, to know which gris-gris or charm was needed.

Though the practice of Voodoo was against the law, and though most of 19th century New Orleans was devoutly Catholic or Protestant, a large part of the population saw no contradiction in asking a Voodoo queen to help fate a little. People from all a walks of life, men and women, rich and poor, black and white came to the Voodoo queens for help. New Orleans newspaper accounts, in the 1800's, referred to Voodoo in serious tones, as if it were generally agreed to have validity. Everyone knew of a neighbor or relative who had experienced some good or evil, that they could attribute to Voodoo. Although those who actually participated in the Voodoo ceremonies were not large in number, those who visited the queens for help, were a huge segment of the population.

Voodoo ceremonies were always held in secret, sometimes in the Queen's back yard, at 1020 St. Ann, or in a hidden place, so as not to attract the authorities. A swampy scene, with moss-hung trees, only added to the other-worldliness of the ceremonies, which usually included her snake, a black cat, a rooster, statues of Catholic saints, holy water, candles and incense.

During the 1800's, as some people moved from New Orleans to other cities up the Mississippi, they took their Voodoo beliefs with them, however unconsciously. There were white Protestants in St. Louis, who would have completely rejected the concept of Voodoo, as totally un-Christian superstition. But, they never missed burying their fingernail clippings or burning the hair from their combs, so that these could not fall into the hands of someone who might use the items to hurt or "control" them.

Marie Laveau died in 1881, but her "throne" remained in the family, as her daughter, by the same name, continued to reign as Voodoo Queen, for many more years. Today, the gravestone of Marie Laveau, in St. Louis Cemetery #1, is still marked with X's, "for good luck." Voodoo continued to be practiced in the city, well into the 1940's. Even in the 1950's, gris-gris and love charms could be found for sale in New Orleans shops.

# MARDI GRAS
## " Throw Me Something Mister ! "
*shout the throngs of spectators, hoping to catch a "throw"*
*from a passing Mardi Gras parade float*

I in New Orleans it is a common joke to say that anything will do as an excuse to have a party. Festivals, here, are just big parties, thrown by the city for itself. Mardi Gras is the biggest party of the year (in a calendar which includes King Cake Parties, St. Joseph's Day, St. Patrick's Day, Jazz Fest, Spring Fiesta, the French Quarter Festival, St John's Eve, Joan of Arc Day, French Bastille Day, the Food Fest, St. Rosalie's Day, the Crawfish Festival, the Strawberry Festival and All Saints' Day) as well as the usual Easter, Memorial Day, 4th of July, Labor Day, Halloween, Thanksgiving and Christmas.

Mardi Gras means "Fat Tuesday" – the last day before Lent begins – the last chance to "eat, drink and be merry." Carnival had been celebrated in Europe for centuries, and Bienville brought the French version with him when he established the colony. But the festivities took their current New Orleans form in 1857, when a group of young men met secretly, to create The Mystick Krewe of Comus, the city's first Carnival Club.

Preparations for the Carnival Season go on all year long – the designing of costumes, ball invitations and parade floats, as well as the elaborate Mardi Gras balls. The actual season begins on

Twelfth Night, soon after Christmas, as the more than 60 Carnival Krewes begin to hold their Masquerade Balls, each with its own King, Queen and full Royal Court. Hundreds of non royal parties are held in offices and homes throughout the city, where King Cakes are served. These large brioche rings, often frosted with the Mardi Gras colors (purple, green and gold) each contain a tiny baby doll. Whoever gets the "baby" in his slice must host the next King Cake party.

Many of the Carnival Clubs also present a parade – the oldest Krewes, through the heart of the city, and some of the newer ones, on routes through

the suburbs. Their themes, costumes and floats are changed each year, and, since the 1960's, each organization has yearly minted its own "doubloons" to throw to the spectators (along with the strings of beads, and other "throws").

Some of the best marching bands in the country (most of which are from New Orleans) march in the parades, giving the crowds good music, to add to the rest of the fun.

In the days before automobiles or electricity, the floats were built on wagons, pulled by satin cloaked mules. At night, the only lighting was provided by men, carrying huge frames of torches, called "Flambeaux." These are still a part of a few parades, and create a truly mysterious atmosphere.

On Mardi Gras Day, the great parades of Zulu and Rex roll through Uptown in the morning. That night, the Kings and Queens of Zulu, Rex and Comus reign over the final balls of the Carnival Season.

The parade-route streets and the French Quarter are full (from morning to night) of costumed revelers, having fun. Some costumes are true works of art, but even the simplest ones, add to the incredible variety and fun, as every one enjoys watching everyone else

There is a private and mysterious side to Mardi Gras, shared only by Krewe members and their guests. But for the public, there are the satin covered horses, the awe inspiring masks, the constant under current of

drumbeats, the nonsense, the colorful and festive atmosphere, the mad scramble for doubloons, the exotic costumes, the community of so many diverse people, all crowded together in fun, and the hope, that maybe this year, you'll catch a Zulu coconut or a glimpse of the Mardi Gras Indians.

Mardi Gras ends at midnight and the party is over. The next day is Ash Wednesday, the first day of Lent (the period for spiritual thoughtfulness and fasting that leads up to Easter).

But even during Lent........there are St. Patrick's Day and St. Joseph's Day to celebrate, each with its own festive parade. And so........the year continues ...........in "The City that Care Forgot."

*Above: "Count" Arnaud Cazenave and his daughter, Germaine, together as King and Queen of Prometheus, in 1938 (Germaine was queen of 22 Mardi Gras Balls-more than any other person. Many of her royal gowns are on display in Arnaud's Restaurant.)*

*Right: A King Cake with traditional Champagne Punch*

*Facing page: Bands that play in the Mardi Gras parades are some of the best in the country.*

*Facing page far right: Some extravagant costumes take the entire year to create*

*Left: The Krewe of Rex parade on Mardis Gras Day, on St. Charles Avenue.*

*Though most of the Carnival organizations base their activities on the romanticized traditions and pageantry of "mock royalty," most have taken these fantasy traditions extremely seriously. In 1910, The Zulu Aid and Pleasure Club was created in the black community. The first King of Zulu wore a "lard can crown" and held a "banana stalk scepter" when he arrived on his "royal barge" (in contrast to the Rex King's "royal yacht" and glittering attire). Since then, Zulu has continued to parade every year (in grass skirts and "black face") and hold its own traditional Mardi Gras ball, always in a spirit of fun.*

# Bad Weather
## *Gone with the wind*

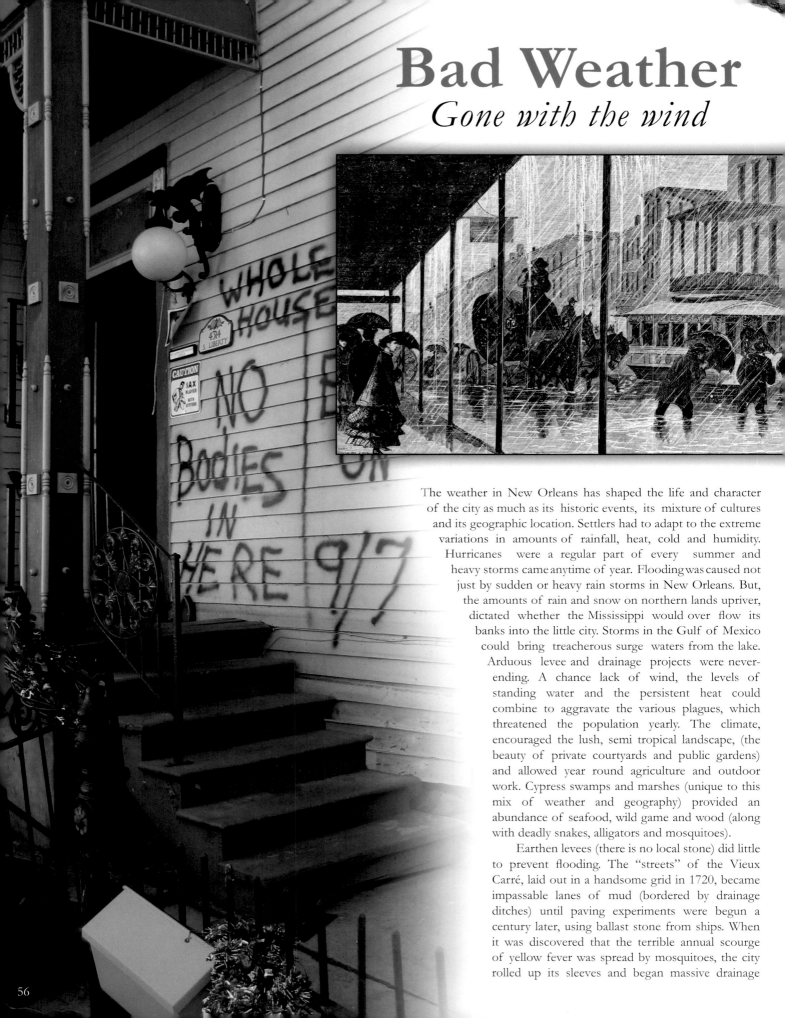

The weather in New Orleans has shaped the life and character of the city as much as its historic events, its mixture of cultures and its geographic location. Settlers had to adapt to the extreme variations in amounts of rainfall, heat, cold and humidity. Hurricanes were a regular part of every summer and heavy storms came anytime of year. Flooding was caused not just by sudden or heavy rain storms in New Orleans. But, the amounts of rain and snow on northern lands upriver, dictated whether the Mississippi would over flow its banks into the little city. Storms in the Gulf of Mexico could bring treacherous surge waters from the lake. Arduous levee and drainage projects were never-ending. A chance lack of wind, the levels of standing water and the persistent heat could combine to aggravate the various plagues, which threatened the population yearly. The climate, encouraged the lush, semi tropical landscape, (the beauty of private courtyards and public gardens) and allowed year round agriculture and outdoor work. Cypress swamps and marshes (unique to this mix of weather and geography) provided an abundance of seafood, wild game and wood (along with deadly snakes, alligators and mosquitoes).

Earthen levees (there is no local stone) did little to prevent flooding. The "streets" of the Vieux Carré, laid out in a handsome grid in 1720, became impassable lanes of mud (bordered by drainage ditches) until paving experiments were begun a century later, using ballast stone from ships. When it was discovered that the terrible annual scourge of yellow fever was spread by mosquitoes, the city rolled up its sleeves and began massive drainage

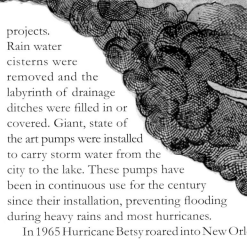

projects.
Rain water cisterns were removed and the labyrinth of drainage ditches were filled in or covered. Giant, state of the art pumps were installed to carry storm water from the city to the lake. These pumps have been in continuous use for the century since their installation, preventing flooding during heavy rains and most hurricanes.

In 1965 Hurricane Betsy roared into New Orleans, with winds of 150 mph and ten feet of surge water through the Gulf Outlet. Overwhelming some levees, the surge deeply flooded parts of the city, including the lower ninth ward (164,000 homes in all). The misery of this storm inspired the strengthening and heightening of most of the city's levees. But evidently this work included "faulty design and inadequate construction," which allowed Hurricane Katrina's surge to overwhelm these "improved" levees in 2005.

Betsy caused over $1billion in damage, not only to homes and businesses, but to ships, port facilities and oil rigs in the Gulf. Katrina's destruction to New Orleans was initially thought to be much less than that of Betsy - it was the failure of the levees, flooding huge sections of the city, which caused Katrina's incredible damage and loss of life.

The city was without power for weeks in the oppressive heat, the deadly contaminated standing water making search efforts or even entry into many neighborhoods impossible. In the first days, neighbors there, risked their lives rescuing others. Then, as authorities prevented return to the city, many sneaked in, surviving with those who had stayed, to begin salvaging their lives, homes and businesses. When they realized that promised help was not on its way, residents started rebuilding, without waiting for government assistance or insurance money, and without the normal sources of food, cleaning or building materials, or needed services (doctors, schools, transportation, hospitals, phones, mail, banks, water or power). Intolerable conditions continued for months, but people persisted in working to rebuild, as best they could. Assistance that did not come from the government was replaced by volunteer help from all over the country. The recovery of New Orleans has mostly been the effort of its own resilient people, determined to save their very special city (with generous help from other Americans, lending a hand).

When the first settlers arrived from France, they encountered a Louisiana landscape, where the water, the marshes and the woods were teeming with wild game, seafood and tropical or unfamiliar plants. Their French cooking tastes and skills had to be adapted to the new ingredients – and the original French cuisine, began its journey toward becoming the Creole cuisine, so distinctive and popular in New Orleans today.

The nearby Choctaw Indians shared their knowledge of gathering and cooking the local plants and animals. The Africans brought their own cooking methods and tastes from West Africa. Their influences in Creole cooking were continuous, since they were most often the ones who presided over the Creole kitchens.

The aristocratic "haute" cuisine and the country farm styles of French cooking were thrown together, influencing each other. In the West Indies, the Spanish and African ways of cooking were modified by new ingredients such as molasses, tropical fruits, spices and peppers. When the Americans (and Irish) arrived, they added their own set of cooking and dining styles to the cuisine. The later immigration of the large Italian population added a rich assortment of their dishes and tastes to the culture.

Much of Creole cuisine is founded on seafood. The oysters from Louisiana waters are considered by most to be the best in the world (and are usually plentiful all year). Oysters on the half shell, on ice, often start the dining experience, and can be followed by a hot platter of any of the cooked oyster preparations, and still just be in the appetizer stage of the meal.

The shrimp and fishing fleets bring in a bounty from the Gulf of Mexico and the surrounding waterways. Shrimp Creole is perhaps the most famous of the myriad of ways that shrimp are prepared in New Orleans. Gumbo is most often made with

# New Orleans' Love Affair with Food
## The Evolution and Traditions of Creole Cuisine

shrimp and other shell fish, and is usually thickened with okra or filé. ("Gombo" was an African word for "okra.") Filé is ground sassafras leaves, and is seldom used *with* okra. Another popular style of Gumbo is a rich combination of chicken (or turkey) and the distinctive local Andouille sausage.

Crawfish and the plentiful local Blue Crabs supply the "meat" for many of the seafood dishes. Crabmeat or crawfish are stuffed into, or put on top of, many other delicacies, both fish and meat. Crabs, themselves are served whole as soft shells, and crawfish are the centerpiece of Crawfish Bisque and Crawfish Étouffée. Crawfish and crabs are often enjoyed just boiled, spicy, and eaten with fingers.

There are so many "traditional" ways to prepare the local fish (red fish, red snapper, pompano, trout and flounder are the most common), and some are very simple preparations. But it sometimes seems Creole chefs have surpassed any normal fish preparations by ladling an already "stuffed" fish with some heavenly sauce, before adding a special crab or shrimp topping.

Many dishes begin with the making of a "roux," and there are endless arguments about how to make this simple combination of flour and oil, fat or butter. After the roux, most of the Creole dishes involve onions, bell peppers, celery, parsley, garlic and tomato. The seasonings can be exotic, and usually have a share of pepper, but most just center on bay leaves, thyme, basil, oregano and lemon.

Vegetables are basic to many dishes. Mirlitons, eggplant and artichokes are often stuffed. Tomatoes were even cultivated into their own "Creole" variety (naturally, considered superior by locals). Pecans are plentiful and are just as likely to top a fish dish, as a dessert. Freshly baked French bread is part of almost every meal.

Rice grew well in the marshy soil and became a staple of Creole cooking. Beans, often regarded elsewhere as a "common" food, were developed into a special dish - Red Beans and Rice, traditionally enjoyed once a week by most New Orleanians, rich and poor. Jambalaya is rice, cooked with various combinations of ham, seafood, vegetables, chicken or sausage — a tasty descendant of the Spanish Paella.

Beef and other meats are served in many distinctive styles, often with classic French sauces. Just as often, the meat is topped or stuffed with a morsel of seafood, or doused and set on fire before serving. Louisiana sausages have their own unique flavors. Turtle soup has long been a favorite of Creoles and alligator has inspired its own appetizers and soups. Frog legs are prepared in several styles.

Huge, flavorful strawberries, as well as oranges, lemons, limes and bananas, all grew in the semi tropical climate, quickly becoming part of recipes for pastries, sauces, mousses, sherbets, drinks and ices.

In 1848, an important local tradition began on a salty piece of earth in South Louisiana. Some peppers, brought from Mexico, were planted, and with the skills of growing and brewing, they became a purely Louisiana taste, used in kitchens in every part of the world –Tabasco Sauce.

But good flavors are only part of the unique dining experience in New Orleans. It's a very complex subject – this city's love affair with food. People here enjoy eating, while standing in a noisy oyster bar, or relish "sucking" the heads and eating the tails of a spicy (and messy) mound of boiled crawfish, spread on newspapers. But they also love experiencing elegance and expert service – the special attention of the same dignified waiter who may have served their father or grandfather. New Orleans can serve you a delicate French sauce, on a perfect fillet of redfish, in a room of white tile and bright lights. Or, you can find red beans and rice, or gumbo, in some of the most elegant surroundings.

From the earliest years, New Orleans became known for its love of food and festivity. Most dining was done in homes, but the traditions which make New Orleans restaurant dining distinctive today, began in the cafés, coffee houses and hotel bars of the Vieux Carré in the early 1800's.

The many coffee houses and bar rooms of the French Quarter were always full of men, who were, over coffee or drinks, conducting business, passionately arguing politics or discussing sugar or cotton prices. In 1834, a northern visitor to New Orleans wrote that in the crowded and noisy coffee houses, every Creole man had a thick cloud of smoke above his head from his large cigar and a glass of sweet liquor punch at his elbow.

Among the cafés, were those with special clienteles. The Café des Réfugees was popular with planters who had fled the revolution in Santo Domingo, while the Café des Exiles attracted aristocrats who had escaped the guillotine in France. At

*Above: Creole dining at Antoine's Restaurant*

*Below: In New Orleans, any excuse for a party will do!*

*Right: Creole Chef Pierre LaCoste with his wife Doralyn (Madame Pierre) with some of his creations from their "Maison Pierre Restaurant" (In the Vieux Carré 1972-1988)*

Maspero's Exchange, a regular group of soldiers, merchants, brokers and newspaper men met daily, to eat, hear the news and transact business. In 1838, Maspero added an auction block and fancy bar to his café. The combination was an instant success.

Across from Maspero's, the huge St. Louis Hotel was built in 1838. Its combined café, bar and auction house was even more successful, especially when the cook began serving a marvelous new concoction called "Gumbo." Then the bar began giving lunch free to drinking customers. This popular idea was soon copied all over the city.

Across St. Louis Street from the hotel, a young man from Marseilles, opened a small "pension" or boarding house. Having been trained in some of Europe's finest kitchens, his skills at adapting the "haute" cuisine of France to the tastes and ingredients of the Creole city, soon made Antoine's famous for simple hospitality and delicious food. In 1868, he moved his famous restaurant to its present location in the next block.

Antoine's dining traditions and recipes have remained intact through five generations. The great, great grandchildren of Antoine, are now serving as the present proprietors, and in turn are training the younger family members in the culinary arts. The unassuming dining rooms have served most of the famous people who have visited New Orleans, and have pleased many generations of her local citizens. Antoine's kitchen invented dishes now common on elegant menus throughout the world (Oysters Rockefeller, for example).

Across from the French Market, another type of Creole café was building a reputation in the 1850's. Madame Begué began cooking large "second" breakfasts (on her wood burning stove) for the butchers and purveyors of the French Market (who had already put in a day's work by mid morning). As word of her good cooking spread, the restaurant became famous for leisurely, elaborate breakfasts (with wines and several courses).

Tujague's Restaurant opened in 1856, a few doors from Madame Begue's and became popular for its tasty cooking, as well. In 1914 the subsequent owners of these two old restaurants combined the Tujague name with the Begué location to form the "new" version of Tujague's. Still popular today, this very traditional restaurant has retained another of New Orleans' dining customs — serving a lunch or dinner of the day, *Table d'Hôte* style.

Jean Galatoire opened his doors in 1905. His same family still attends to every detail of the operation of this famous restaurant. In this city, many budding *restaurateurs* are sent by their parents to study cooking and wine in France, before receiving a position in the family restaurant.

Galatoire's is proud of the generations of regular customers, both locals and those who visit New Orleans frequently. Famous for both a festive atmosphere and an absolute insistence on tradition in food and service, this grand restaurant personifies what is special about New Orleans dining.

The colorful story of Arnaud's began when "Count" Arnaud Cazenave opened his doors in 1918. Under both flamboyant father and daughter, it was popular for over fifty years, as one of the premier dining locales in the city. It was restored to its former glory by a new owner, Archie Casbarian, in the 1980's, and continues now with the recipes and distinctive character that made it famous. The "Jazz Brunch" is a festive tradition, enjoyed here, as well.

In 1920, Joseph Broussard began his restaurant in the handsome 1824 building on Rue Conti. Broussard's became famous for its French Creole food and its large, beautiful courtyard. The Pruess family is today continuing Broussard's dining traditions and fine French Creole cuisine. Diners in their lovely courtyard enjoy the century old wisteria vine which blooms each spring.

Brennan's, perhaps the youngest of the "old" Vieux Carré restaurants, was opened in 1946 by a New Orleanian from the "Irish Channel" area of Uptown. He had been challenged by "Count" Arnaud, that an Irishman couldn't run a fine French Creole restaurant. He created and ran one as fine as any in the city ! Brennan's moved in 1950 from Bourbon Street to the unusual 1801 Casa Faurie on Royal. The Creole custom of long, leisurely and elaborate breakfasts was made most famous here.

Brennan's too, offers patio dining in one of the beautiful old lush courtyards of the French Quarter. Other members of the Brennan family have opened such respected newer Vieux Carré restaurants as Mr. B's, the Palace Café, Red Fish Grill and Bacco.

Some of the more casual, but respected, "old timers" in the French Quarter, include the Gumbo Shop (1795 building) and the Napoleon House (run by the same family in this historic building since 1914). Not far away, on Canal (in Mid City) Mandina's has been serving Creole specialties to a loyal local crowd, since the Mandina family opened their restaurant in late 1800's.

Several current restaurants have been an important part of life on the American side

*"In the French Market," detail from a painting by William Woodward,*
*from the collection of Mr. and Mrs. James W. Nelson.*
*William Woodward taught at Newcomb College and Tulane University,*
*and he and his brother Ellsworth were important figures*
*in the art community of New Orleans, from 1884 to 1939.*

of the city, for many years. Maylie's was serving the butchers of the Poydras Market 1876. Other respected old establishments in the Central Business District, include the Bon Ton, The Sazerac and Mother's.

In 1880, Émile Commander opened his popular Commander's Palace in a dramatic Victorian mansion in the heart of the Garden District. Later, members of the Brennan family became proprietors of this Creole Restaurant, and have made its fine cuisine and garden atmosphere famous. Many fine chefs have come into their own at Commanders, encouraged in creating new traditions. Another of New Orleans' dining traditions has been popular here - a gourmet and festive Jazz Brunch, under the huge oak branches of their large courtyard.

Delmonico began its good reputation in 1895, and Pascal Manale's has been in the same family since 1913. Other popular "old" Uptown restaurants include The

Upperline, the Camilia Grill, Uglesich and Casamentos.

The exciting evolution of New Orleans' distinctive cooking and dining is not something limited just to the past. In recent years, such chefs as Paul Prudhomme, Alex Patout, John Folse and Emeril Lagasse have become widely known for their creative additions to the cuisine and show off their expertise in their own restaurants. Chef Austin Leslie even inspired a TV series about his Creole-soul food restaurant in New Orleans. Ruth's Chris Steak Houses and Popeyes Chicken were both born in the Crescent City.

An unusual contributor to the development of the distinctive cuisine was the character of the early markets. Along the riverbank, in sight of the many ships from distant ports, the Indians' displayed their herbs, roots, filé and baskets for the French settlers. The early German farmers

*Right: At Galatoire's, dining tradition and fine Creole food are a long-standing legacy.*

*Below: The unique building of Commander's Palace Restaurant in the Garden District*

*Left: "The Oyster Wagon" New Orleans watercolor by Tommy Thompson*

brought their produce and dairy products to sell. The "French" Market, from its very beginning, was a center for a diversity of products from all over the world.

There were buildings erected to house the butchers, the vegetable stalls and other common commodities, but these were soon surrounded by an assortment of canopies, stalls and blankets on the ground, for selling every description of cooking ingredients or prepared refreshments.

The Market was crammed with people from early morning – sellers with their wares, and women, children and servants carrying large baskets to fill. Voices could be heard of women and salesmen bartering the prices or quality of goods, vendors hollering out their specials, sailors and soldiers, and every level of conversation and argument, carried on in French, "Patois," English, Spanish, German and more. Added to these, were the sounds of chickens, parrots and other caged birds, monkeys for sale and perhaps a brass band or organ grinder in the background. In the second century of its history, the sound of the steamboat whistles was a constant backdrop to the already noisy market.

Smells of every kind mingled and contrasted – the pungent thick smell of steaming coffee, the sweet fragrances of freshly baked pies, mlasses, pralines, spices and fruits and the sharp odors of fish and oysters. Live chickens hung in bunches by their feet, mules stood waiting with the wagons alongside, and the butchers' stalls were notoriously dirty.

The market attracted all sorts of con men, entertainers and cure-all salesmen. Live alligators were displayed and there was even a dentist, who would "perform" tooth pulling, for all to watch.

Sundays were especially festive at the Market. After morning Mass, Creole famil) lies would shop for the big Sunday dinner to be prepared, enjoying the excursion through the Market as a festive family outing. At first, the mostly Protestant Americans (usually discouraged from any work, commerce or festivity on the Sabbath) were shocked at the gaiety and bustle of the Creoles' French Market.

In 1838, the American sector established its own Poydras Market. Busy and similarly picturesque, it served the Central Business District for almost a hundred years.

Stuffing a loaf of French bread with tasty combinations of seafood, meats or sausage, Po'Boys can make an inexpensive meal. When the many Italian families opened stores and cafés along the streets which bordered the French Market in the late 1800's, they served Po'Boys and Muffalettas (special freshly baked loaves, filled with meats, cheeses and olive salad) and began the endless local arguments as to who makes the best of these sandwiches. The Italian grocery stores along Decatur also sell many other Italian food items.

Even into the 1950's, it was a common in New Orleans, to see black women, carrying large baskets or wooden bowls, expertly balanced on their heads. They would walk the streets, singing out (usually in French) the names of the treats they were selling.

The woman who called out, "Belle calas – tout chaud," was selling hot freshly made sweet rice fritters for breakfast tables. Untilrecent years, one could always find a Praline Lady, sitting in a doorway, with her large basket of sweet pralines she had made. Blackberry Ladies or Vegetable Ladies would pick their produce in the morning and walk the streets, selling to those who did not go to market. Coffee, cheeses, pies, cakes and sandwiches were all sold this way.

There were also men and boys, selling many similar products from baskets or carts. Milk was poured into housewives' (or restaurants') pitchers from large milk cans on wagons. Waffle Men sold hot, sugar coated waffles and water carts dispensed Mississippi River "drinking" water. The arrival of the Snowball Man was eagerly awaited, with his syrup covered shaved ice – so refreshing in the hot climate. (Snowballs are still a favorite treat in New Orleans.) Ice was a rare commodity (before refrigeration). It was brought down the river on barges in the spring, from frozen lakes in the north. Except for snowballs, ice was usually purchased only by the wealthy, for Mint Juleps, sorbets and other upper class treats.

The "Roman Candy Man" began driving his mule and wagon through the streets of New Orleans in 1915, cooking his special "chewing candy" on a little burner. His grandson took over, in 1972, driving the mule and wagon through the modern streets, but making his grandfather's candy in the same old way. In New Orleans, few people want to let go of tradition.

In this city, the selection, preparation and serving of good food are regarded as serious and respected arts. French cooking was transformed through the years into a truly distinctive cuisine, and "enjoyment" is considered to be an important part of life. The city loves its dining traditions and its food,

*Above:*
*The* main *dining room of Arnaud's, serving French Creole specialties since 1918*

*Left:*
*Seafood gumbo is usually made with either okra or filé powder*

# The Grand Avenues
## St. Charles and Canal

When the little walled city of New Orleans began to expand in the 1770's, the Gravier Plantation, which lay across Canal, was divided into lots, forming the Faubourg St. Marie. In 1803, the Americans, flooding into the city and snubbed by the Creole population, quickly made the new suburb into a thriving "American" community.

The poor began settling mostly along the busy river, while successful merchants and brokers began building grand homes in the Coliseum Square area. By the 1820's, competition between the Creoles and the newcomers was fierce. The Creole majority on the city council refused to vote for such improvements as wharves, street paving or wharfs on the American side of Canal.

So, just outside the city limit, beyond Coliseum Square, a new American community was incorporated as Lafayette City in 1833, whose beautiful homes and yards became known as the Garden District.

New Orleans was run as three separate municipalities: the Vieux Carré, the City of Lafayette and the area downriver from the Vieux Carré, until 1852, when these competing areas were reunited as one city. Meanwhile, the Anglos were slowly building homes further along the entire length of their grand St. Charles Avenue.

Canal Street remained the unofficial dividing line (the neutral ground) during the 1800's, between the old Creole Vieux Carré and the more "American" sections that eventually became known as the "Central Business District" (or CBD) and "Uptown."

Canal Street is one of the widest streets in the world. It was named, unromantically, for a drainage canal that was to border the Vieux Carré. At the foot of the street, is the dock for the free Canal Street Ferry, which can take you (with or without a vehicle) across the Mississippi (2,200 feet wide here) to the "West Bank" town of Algiers. Until the building of the Huey P. Long Bridge in 1935, ferries were the only way to cross the River (even for trains – one car at a time).

*Top right: Postcard of 1960 Canal Street*

*Far right: The Latter Library on St. Charles Ave.*

*Lower right: The St. Charles streetcar*

*Below: Canal Street, one of the widest avenues in the world. Still a thriving commercial street, it divides the Vieux Carré from the Central Business District and runs from the River to the Lake.*

Also, at the foot of Canal is a modern marvel, the Aquarium of the Americas, with fascinating displays of marine life. It stands about where one of five forts guarded the city during the 1700's.

In the 400 block of Canal Street is the old US Customs House. Henry Clay laid the cornerstone for this massive building in 1847. Its construction, interrupted by the Civil War, took 34 years to complete. The huge interior columns are supported by a grid of cypress logs below the ground.

In the eleventh block of Canal is the Saenger Theater. Now a Performing Arts Center, it was built in 1927, in the era of grand movie houses. Its dramatic ceiling was a dark sky full of twinkling stars and its lobby was lined with statues.

Life in the new American part of town was centered along St. Charles Avenue, where the St. Charles Streetcar still runs. Laid out in the 1796 plan for Faubourg St. Marie, was the little "park" called Lafayette Square, in the fifth block of St. Charles. It was the Americans' answer to the Creoles' Jackson Square. Near it, they built their important civic buildings, churches, hotels and the St. Charles Theater (finest in the U.S., during the 1830's).

*The Warehouse District lies along the River near Canal. These buildings used to house much of the commerce and shipping of the busy port. Now, the area is being revitalized, as some of the old, empty structures are being renovated for a variety of modern uses.*

*St. Patrick's Church, at 712 Camp, was begun in 1838, serving mostly the Irish Catholics, who were unhappy with the St.Louis Cathedral, in the Vieux Carré, "where God spoke only French."*

*Above: Postcard of the St. Charles Hotel, 1920's*

*Below: Gallier Hall on St. Charles across from Lafayette Square.*

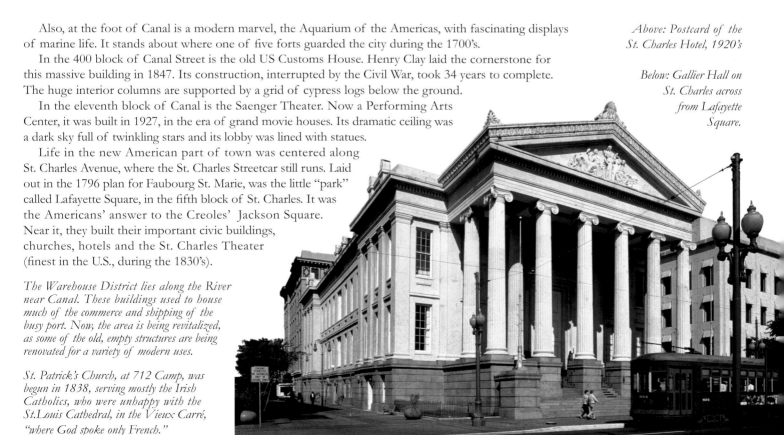

A block away from St. Charles, at 231 Carondelet, was the old Cotton Exchange, where cotton factors and merchants met to regulate prices and facilitate trade. When French Impressionist painter Edgar Degas visited his mother's family in New Orleans, in 1872-1873, he painted "a typical day of the gentlemen at The Cotton Office."

In 1842, the first version of the St. Charles Hotel was finished in the second block of St. Charles, as the Americans' grand rival to the St. Louis Hotel of the Vieux Carré. Its huge dome was a landmark, visible for miles. Wealthy visitors were accommodated in luxurious comfort. The grand hotel was the center of social and business affairs in the American side of town. It burned and was rebuilt twice. It was torn down in 1974 (photo page 69).

In 1850, the new City Hall (now called Gallier Hall, after its designer, architect James Gallier, Sr.) was built on Lafayette Square, for the American Municipality. It later served as City Hall for the entire city, until 1957, when the new Civic Center was built. Each year the King and Queen of Carnival are toasted in front of Gallier Hall.

Lee Circle was designed to be "Place du Tivoli," a cultural center with a carousel in the middle. Although the plan was never completed, all the streets nearby had been given names from mythology. In 1883, when the statue of Robert E. Lee was dedicated, both the Confederate President Jefferson Davis and General Beauregard were among the guests of honor. On Lee Circle, is the Confederate Memorial Hall, opened in 1891, which displays uniforms, artifacts and weapons from the Civil War.

At 1508 St. Charles, stands the Connery House. Built in 1847, it was originally a traditional Greek Revival House, but was extensively remodeled in 1896 in the Queen Anne Style (its galleries replaced with a turret and bay windows).

The Greek Revival house at 2220 St. Charles, was the home built for George Washington Squires in 1851. After crossing Jackson Avenue, St. Charles becomes one border of the Garden District. At 2265, the unusually fine Greek Revival house was built in 1856, with the large inheritance of Miss Lavinia Dabney. She lost her fortune in the recession of the following year, and was forced to sell the new house (photo page 72).

The raised cottage at 2524 St. Charles, was built in 1856 for Mrs. Louise Claiborne de Marigny (from prominent American *and* Creole families). An undertaker, Frances Johnson, gained sufficient wealth to have the Queen Anne style home, at 2727 constructed for him in 1891.

*"Raised cottage" is the term given to an early style of Louisiana house. Copied from the West Indies, it was designed for the tropical climate. The house was raised off the soggy ground (and above any flood waters). The roof extended to cover galleries, front and back. Galleries protected the walls and French windows from the hot sun and torrential rains and helped catch as much breeze as was possible.*

*"Greek Revival" was a style which swept Southern architecture in the early 19th century. Pillars and capitals, cornices and pediments, and many other Greek elements and motifs were dominant in the designs.*

*"Queen Anne" architecture became popular in New Orleans in the late 1800's. It involved the heavy use of decorative trim (usually painted wood - not iron) "gingerbread" towers, gables, bay windows, and ornate porches.*

*Above: The Claiborne de Marigny House (an elegant raised cottage) 2524 St. Charles*

*Far Left: The bronze sculpture of Confederate hero Robert E. Lee stands on a one hundred foot pillar in the center of Lee Circle*

*Left: A modern day vegetable and fruit vendor, among the elegant homes along St. Charles Ave.*

*Right: A Greek Revival home at 2344 St Charles with galleries on the side as well as the front. These gave the house light and ventilation within, and settings for the enjoyment of garden views and river breezes on sultry days.*

*Below: The fine
Greek Revival House
of Lavinia Dabney,
2265 St. Charles
(story, previous page)*

*Above: The massive
Brown mansion,
4717 St. Charles*

*Left: The Wedding Cake
House, 5809 St. Charles
(story, following page)*

*In the
Uptown area
was the home
of Captain
Thomas P.
Leathers.
In 1870, he
was at the wheel
of the Steamboat
Natchez, during
the famous
riverboat race
with the
Robert E. Lee
between New
Orleans and
St. Louis.
He spent 57
years on the
Mississippi.
His son was
also a captain,
whose very
unusual wife
Blanche became
an accomplished
steamboat
captain as well.*

The mansions at 2503 and 2525, were built for high-rollers in 1885 and 1890. Col. Joseph Walker owned gambling houses and his own bank, while John Morris was an educated, wealthy New Jersey gambler, with horse tracks and a major interest in the infamous Louisiana Lottery of 1886-1892.

Thomas McDermott built the Italianate house at 2926 St. Charles, in 1882. For year round comfort, it has a 12 inch space between inner and outer walls and a gallery or balcony for every room. The wealthy commission merchant, Richard Flower, constructed his home at 3005, in the newly popular "Second Empire" style in 1874.

At 3029, Civil War Captain Watson Van Benthuysen built his grand house in 1869, with the fortune he had made as an industrialist and merchant. From 1931 to 1941, the house was used as the German Consulate. From here, Consul Adolf Peck-elsheim secretly informed Axis submarines about ship departures from New Orleans.

The elaborate mansion at 3811 St. Charles was built by a cigar manufacturer, Simon Hernsheim, in 1884. It was used as one of the sets for the movie "Pretty Baby."

In 1887, Les Mesdames de Sacre Coeur began their prominent Catholic girls school, Sacred Heart Academy, their handsome campus at 4521 St. Charles erected in 1899.

Cotton merchant William Brown built the enormous mansion at 4717 St. Charles for his new bride in 1902. Though most of the plantations near New Orleans were planted in sugar cane, one third of the cotton, grown in the United States, came through the port of New Orleans. Many vast fortunes were made in the brokering, factoring, storing, insuring and shiping of that cotton.

Another Second Empire style house, at 4803 St. Charles, was constructed for Joseph Hernandez, President of the Streetcar Line in the 1890's. At 4920, stands a 1910 re-creation of plantation grandeur, built by John Dantzler, who was a wealthy lumber magnate.

Built by Col. William Lewis in 1868, as a wedding gift to his daughter, the unusual mansion at 5005 St. Charles was remodeled in 1927. It has been occupied since 1925, by the Orleans Club, a private women's "social and cultural" club.

The Milton Latter Memorial Library, at 5120 St. Charles, was donated to the City in

*Above: The Orleans Club, 5005 St. Charles*

*Above: Dominican College, 7214 St. Charles (story page 75)*

1948, as a memorial to a son lost in WWII. Built in 1907, the home had at one time belonged to silent film star, Marguerite Clark.

Two unusual, Mansard roofed houses, in the 5600 block of St. Charles, add a French touch to this American Avenue. In the next block, at 5700, is a 1941 home, built as a copy of Tara, Scarlet O'Hara's plantation home in Gone with the Wind. But, the original Tara was actually only a creation of the movie set designer !

Peacefully shrouded in trees at 5800 St. Charles, stand two Italianate raised cottages built in 1870 and 1867. At 5809, the ornate mansion is nicknamed the Wedding Cake House, for its decorative garlands and pillared tiers. Built in 1896, it has beautiful stained glass windows on its uptown side.

Continuing up St. Charles, most of the huge mansions along the lakeside of the street, were built in the early 1900's. The house at 6000, was one of the finest designs of Architect Thomas Sully, in 1895.

Loyola University's Marquette Hall, at 6363, was built in 1904, when the Jesuits founded this Roman Catholic school. Their Church of the Holy Name was built in 1914

Next door, at 6823, is Tulane University. Beginning as a Medical College, near Canal Street, in 1834, the school moved to this location in 1882, upon receiving a huge gift from prosperous businessman, Paul Tulane. Gibson Hall was built the following year. Newcomb College is the Women's College of Tulane. Founded in 1886, by the very wealthy Josephine Newcomb, it has long been famous for its Art School.

Spacious Audubon Park was established across from Tulane, in 1884, on the grounds of the old sugar plantation of

*Above: The main entrance of Audubon Park. The park spreads over 340 acres of ancient moss draped live oak trees, winding lagoons and trails, the world class Audubon Zoo, public recreation facilities and a great river view along the levee.*

*Right: The Tulane Presidents' House at the corner of Audubon Place and St.Charles Avenue*

Etienne de Boré. It was this prominent Creole, who in 1795, was the first planter to successfully granulate cane sugar. He and most of his neighbors were facing ruin, having lost their Indigo crops to a worm epidemic. They all then replanted in sugar cane, and began the profitable sugar industry, that helped make the city so rich.

The Great Cotton Exposition of 1884-1885 was held on these grounds, attracting thousands of visitors to New Orleans and the "New South." Many of the ancient trees which shade the park are members of the Live Oak Society. They have "names" and are each protected by law.

Audubon Place is a private drive, built in 1894, and nicknamed "Millionaires' Row." Where Audubon Place meets St. Charles Ave., is an enormous pillared mansion, built in 1907. It was later bought by Samuel Zemurray, Chairman of the United Fruit Company. Though he began as a poor immigrant youth, he willed this grand house to Tulane, to be the home of its presidents.

At 7214 St. Charles stands an exotic old building, Greenville Hall, built in 1887, as part of Dominican College. Beginning as a girls' boarding school, in 1865, Dominican became a college in 1910. Closed in the 1980's, its campus is now owned by Loyola.

At the end of St. Charles Avenue, the road turns abruptly and becomes Carrollton Avenue. This sharp angle is forced by the bend of the Mississippi River close by, and the area is called The Riverbend. The tiny town of Carrollton began here, as a resort destination of the early streetcar line, and was later absorbed into New Orleans. The Levee, working to hold back the mighty Mississippi, is visible here, near the road.

*John James Audubon's* Birds of America, *were volumes of paintings (and written text) of almost five hundred species of birds in their natural settings. A scientist-naturalist, as well as an accomplished painter, Audubon made many of his paintings, while living in New Orleans during 1821 and 1822.*

# The St. Charles Streetcar
## The oldest continuously operating streetcar in the world.

Rumbling along the *neutral ground* of St. Charles and Carrollton Avenues for more than 150 years, the streetcar has become a treasured symbol of the New Orleans, as well as a practical and romantic means of transportation. The mahogany seats, brass fittings and exposed ceiling light bulbs are from a day before plastic and aluminum were even thought of.

The route forms a 13.2 mile crescent (following the curve of the River) from Canal Street, along majestic St. Charles as it leads through "Uptown" to Carrollton. Turning with the "Riverbend," it travels Carrollton to the end of the line at Claiborne. Here, it used to connect with all the other streetcar lines, which rolled through the city on a vast web of track. Now this, the oldest route, reverses direction, to carry its mixture of tourists, uptown residents, commuters and school children back toward downtown.

It was the St. Charles street car, which first made possible the development of the *suburban* Garden District. As the tremendous river commerce boomed in the early 1800's, fortunes were made in the shipping of sugar, cotton and commodities needed by the growing city and expanding nation. Successful businessmen now wanted to live in the quiet, safer, spacious land further up river from the congested business district where they worked. The convenient rail transportation made this commuting practical in a time when St. Charles Avenue was a muddy trail, cut with a patchwork of deep ruts. It wasn't until the 1880's, that this roadway along the tracks was converted into the grand paved boulevard we enjoy today.

In 1835, the New Orleans and Carrollton Railroad began operation of the St. Charles Streetcar Line, then called the Carrollton Line. Steam powered cars from England traveled from Canal Street, through the *faubourgs* (suburbs) upriver to the tiny resort town of Carrollton.

Shortly after the Civil War, ex-Confederate General P.G.T. Beauregard leased the NO & CRR, and did away with the steam locomotives, reverting to horse power. The horse drawn streetcars, though inefficient, provided a quieter citywide network of transportation. Horse drawn cars lasted for more than 20 years, despite attempts to replace them with technology such as ammonia powered engines, steam dummy engines, cables and electric batteries.

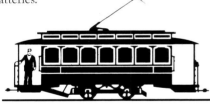

Finally, in 1893, the first cars that used overhead electricity went into operation. The new electric cars were built by the St. Louis Car Co. and a gala celebration was held to mark the installation of the system, which continues to serve the line today.

In 1922, a complete reorganization of all power companies and street railways led to the New Orleans Public Service taking over the operation of the streetcars. In 1923, the current streetcar, which was designed and built by the Perley A. Thomas Car Company, was introduced into service.

Beginning in the 1930's, streetcars were gradually replaced by buses, which were considered faster and more comfortable by some. The phasing out continued until 1964, when the Canal Street Line was shut down, leaving only the St. Charles Line. With the closing of the Canal Line, 11 of the cars were sold to various museums across the country.

In 1984, the "Bring Our Streetcars Home" Committee (BOSH) was formed to reclaim some of the cars sold in 1964. All 11 cars were located and three were bought and returned to the Crescent City in late 1985. Two of these cars have been renovated and put into operation on the Riverfront line, New Orleans' first new streetcar line since 1926. Now the Canal Street Line is also back in operation in the center of the wide neutral ground.

The St. Charles Line was named to the National Register of Historic Places in 1973. In 1984, the line was declared a National Historic Mechanical Engineering Landmark.

These classic streetcars were originally designed for operation by a motorman at the front, who drove the car, and a conductor at the rear, who collected fares and directed passengers. However, when electric fareboxes were installed in 1970, the conductor's function became unnecessary, so the streetcars were adapted for one-man operation.

Our streetcars do not turn around at the end of the line. Instead, the operator transfers control from one end of the car to the other. When the operator reaches the end of the line, he raised the "front" trolley pole. He then makes his way to the other end of the car and lowers what was the "rear" trolley pole. It is always the rear trolley that conducts the 600 volts of current to the two motors.

*How They Work:*
*The operator handles the control points and the brakes with two hand controls. The compressed air braking system is the most difficult function to master. The "clunkity-clunk-clunk," heard at different times, is the air compressor, pumping air into the pressure tank reservoir.*

*The brakes must be pumped gradually for a smooth stop, and require a great distance for stopping. (Think twice before stepping or pulling out in front of a moving streetcar.)*

Year Built: 1923-24  Place: Hight Point, NC
Seating Capacity: 52 Weight: 42,000 pounds
Maximum Speed: 28 mph
Power: 65-hp electric motor
Dimensions: Length-47'8"  Width-7'10"

# The Garden District

At the time the American newcomers were moving up river, from the business district and the Creole dominated government, the old Livaudais Plantation, above Coliseum Square, was sold for development. The Americans soon began buying lots and building their elegant homes, in what came to be called the Garden District. *They* called the area the City of Lafayette, incorporating it in 1833.

Some of these early newcomers had been immigrants to the United States, before New Orleans had become an American city. Many had come from poverty and saw business as their opportunity for success.

During the first half of the 19th Century, the port was a world of opportunity, and the new businessmen had the drive to sell, broker, factor, finance, insure, ship, package or warehouse almost any commodity. Business just thrived. A Frenchman visiting New Orleans in 1850 observed, New Orleans "is a world of commission men, speculators and dealers, who argue feverishly in the midst of their piled up merchandise."

As many of the Anglo businessmen became successful, built their homes and families, and gained the prestige and power that came with their wealth, they began to adopt aspects of the old city's culture. The "Northern" passion for business began to mellow to the Creoles' more leisurely life style and enjoyment of everyday pleasures. French customs, culture and terminology began to be adopted as "Southern," rather than "foreign." As they became New Orleanians, they began to view the South more romantically, as the "natural" and rightful order of things. Business became only one part of their more genteel attitude and lifestyle. The luxurious homes they built, reflected their embrace of an idealized South.

*Above: The huge Buckner Mansion, 1410 Jackson*

# The Garden District

The Creoles were the ones who dubbed the area the "Garden District," noting the beautiful lawns and lush gardens, which surrounded the new homes. (In the Creole Vieux Carré, gardens were in private courtyards, hidden from the street behind high walls.) In the Garden District, fences were just enough to keep out wandering cattle, but made of open iron work, to allow the house and grounds to be seen.

Many of the early houses of the Garden District were on enormous lots, as whole blocks were divided into only four. In a few cases, wealthy buyers took an entire block for a single residence. This generous land encouraged the spacious gardens and grand scale of the architecture. Most of the original lots were divided and sold in later years, as fortunes rose and fell.

The Garden District begins at Jackson Avenue, nicknamed "Bragg Boulevard," during the 1850's, when it was lined with many of the early grand homes. Ironically, *it* is the street that has lost more of its old mansions than any other. Even so, there are still many fascinating houses left on Jackson Avenue.

At the corner of Jackson and Prytania, an ornate, raised cottage faces Prytania at 2127. This house was built by wealthy cotton broker Alexander Harris, in 1857. The great oaks on the property were planted in 1874, "the day the Carpetbaggers left New Orleans."

In 1859, the building at 1452 Jackson was constructed to be a pharmacy below, with the family's living quarters above. Pope's Pharmacy became a popular meeting place for "The Club." Rich Garden District residents, like Henry Buckner and John Burnside, would gather on benches in front, to discuss politics and business.

Cotton broker and merchant, Henry Buckner, had first lived in Faubourg St. Marie, and then built homes in the Coliseum Square area. In 1856, his business partner built a grand mansion in Natchez. Not to be outdone, Buckner had his 48 column house designed, at 1410 Jackson, with 22,000 square feet of living space. From 1923 to 1983, the huge house was used as Soulé College, but it then became a private home again.

At 1435 Jackson, Mrs. Hattie Thorn had her raised cottage built in 1883, for $7,550. The large home at 1411, which William Perkins built in 1850, combined Italinate features with the Greek Revival style, more

*"Carriage stones" are the large, flat granite blocks, seen near the curb in front of some houses. These were for helping with the tall step into, or out of, the high wheeled carriages.*

*The New Orleans Museum of Art, in City Park, has a large permanent collection, specializing in African and pre-Columbian art. Local, American and European masters are well represented, and the museum has been host to major international exhibits, as well.*

common to early Garden District homes.

Trinity Church was built at 1329 Jackson, in 1851 - an Episcopal church, to serve the mostly Protestant Americans of the Garden District. Bishop Polk was a West Point graduate, before he became a Bishop and Rector of Trinity Church. At Jefferson Davis' request, Polk "buckled the sword over the gown" and became a Major General in the Confederate Army. He was killed fighting, in 1864. The devoted women of his congregation saved his extensive library in the church, from the occupying Union troops, by smuggling the books out under their hoop skirts.

At 1236 Jackson, George Sweet replaced his home with a grander Italianate one, in 1874. He was a wholesale grocer and the proprietor of the huge St. Charles Hotel.

The raised cottage at 1224 Jackson was built about 1860, for the Swain family (photo, following page). Its curving gallery is unusual, as it follows the lines of the front bay. A large wing that originally stood behind the house, burned in the 1950's.

Luther Stewart was another wholesale grocer, who became wealthy supplying goods to the booming population. He built the home at 1208 Philip, in 1858.

The widowed Madame Tureaud had the

house at 1220 Philip constructed for her during the 1850's. It was later bought by Samuel Delgado, a prosperous dealer in sugar and molasses. The Delgados raised their nephew Isaac in the house.

Isaac Delgado entered his uncle's sugar business at an early age and, with several other businesses, he became very wealthy. He later gave his extensive art collection to be the nucleus for the New Orleans Museum of Art. He also left money for the creation of Delgado College and several city hospitals.

At 1223 Philip, is a structure, which had been the carriage house of a much larger home, that had stood to the right. During the 1930's, two elderly sisters, the Misses Butler, had bought the carriage house. When visiting from the plantation their family had owned since 1800, they enjoyed their lush garden and the Garden District neighborhood of their little "town house."

At 1239 Philip, Samuel Trufant replaced an earlier house, in 1891, with one that was very different in style from its Greek Revival neighbors.

Almost identical to *its* neighbor, is the

*Above: The Swain House (raised cottage) 1224 Jackson (story, previous page) Right: The Grinnan Villa, 2221 Prytania*

*Ditches with bridges lined both sides of Garden District streets. These were the means of drainage for the heavy rainfall as well as the house hold dishwater. For all the elegance of the Garden District, these ditches, often choked with debris, standing water and mosquitoes, were a primitive contrast.*

Greek Revival house of John Rodenberg, at 1238 Philip, constructed in 1853. The wall are 18 inches thick and the ceilings, 14 feet high. Rodenberg was a dealer in grains and feed. The house was later owned, for fifty years, by the David Pipes family and was admired for its beautiful gardens. In his later years, Pipes was quoted as having said, "I attended college in Mississippi, but I graduated from Lee's Army at Appomatox." His father had fought in the Battle of New Orleans.

A row of small houses at 2305-2329 Coliseum, was given the nickname, "The Seven Sisters," due to the myth that they were commissioned by a father, to be wedding presents for his daughters. Actually, they were constructed by an architect, in 1868, on speculation. A great view of the rear galleries and service wing of the huge Buckner Mansion (on Jackson) is visible from this block.

In 1855, Florence Luling either built or remodeled the raised cottage at 1433 Philip. Later, Luling became extremely wealthy from his commercial enterprises during the Civil War, and built a colossal home on Esplanade Avenue.

The dignified Italianate villa, at 2221 Prytania, was designed by the Irish born, Henry Howard, for the London born, Robert Grinnan. Arriving in New Orleans, in 1850, Grinnan was so successful as a cotton broker and commission merchant, that he began this villa that same year.

A more modest Italianate villa stands at 2320 Prytania. It was built for E.K. Bryant, who was also a prosperous cotton merchant in the years before the Civil War.

The raised cottage at 2340 Prytania is probably the oldest house in the Garden District. Standing alone for many years, it was called, "Toby's Corner." It was constructed for Thomas Toby in 1838. He was both a wheelwright and commission merchant, and introduced a successful style of dray (wagon) for hauling cotton. Descendants of the family have lived here for several generations.

"Texas Toby" was the name given to one of Toby's eleven children. A passionate supporter of the struggle for Texas Independence, he sank his fortunes into that cause. Later, when he was near bankruptcy, he appealed to the new country of Texas to repay his advances, but to no avail. Upon his death, his belongings were auctioned to pay his debts.

Bradish Johnson was one of those who prospered during the hard times of Reconstruction. In 1872, wealth from his sugar plantations built the stately French Second Empire style house at 2343 Prytania. It was the most extravagant and costly home in the District at the time. In 1929, Louise McGehee moved her private girls school into the building. Eventually, the carriage house became a gym and the stables, a cafeteria. For more than 70 years, girls have been climbing Johnson's grand curved staircase to their classrooms above.

Many Uptown homes have been used as Consulates, in the port city of New Orleans. The French Consulate has long been the resident of the house at 2406 Prytania.

*Left: Bradish Johnson House (McGehee School) 2343 Prytania*

*The Livaudais Oak is the huge tree on Toby's Corner, named for the plantation on which the Garden District was built. It is a member of the Live Oak Society. The towering magnolias were planted in the 1830's or before.*

*There is a reverence for trees in this city, as sidewalks, curbs and fences are all adjusted to accommodate the spreading roots and branches of the live oaks and magnolias. Normally, large branches are cut, only when they pose a danger, not an inconvenience.*

*The cast iron "wheel guards" (still standing patrol at some driveways in the District) were designed for carriage wheels, but still prevent an occasional car tire in the ditch, today.*

# The Garden District

The very large, double galleried home at 1420 First Street, has both Greek Revival and Italianate features.

In the next block, the house at 1312 First Street was built in 1849, as a modest raised cottage, with a front gallery, facing Chestnut. In 1877, it was transformed, as the building was moved to face First, and raised up to become the second floor and attic of the present home (a new first floor being added below). The new bays and Italianate facade were attached in the style popular in the 1870's.

Across the street, at 1331 First, Architect Samuel Jamison designed this house in 1869, during the difficult years after the Civil War. Joseph Morris was a dealer in cordage, whose post-war business was sufficient to have this grand home constructed. (A later owner of the house sold the large garden, where a newer, more modern home now stands.)

Designed in the same year, by the same architect, the house at 1315 First was the pride of Joseph Carroll, a very prosperous cotton factor from Virginia. The interior was created with rosewood and mahogany moldings, Italian marble mantles and crystal chandeliers. Lavish parties were given here, which included such guests as painter Edgar Degas and writer Mark Twain. The unusual galleries were cast in New Orleans.

Around the corner, at 2339 Chestnut, is the Carriage House of the Carroll mansion (on First). This picturesque building housed the carriages downstairs and the groom in the quarters above. The horses would have been unhitched and taken to stables at the back of the property or to a livery stable nearby.

A "factor" was a type of speculator-broker-financier all in one. In order to handle the sale of a crop of cotton or sugar for a plantation, the "factor" sometimes had to first supply the very scarce capital needed to plant it. Often, with crop failure or price recession, the mortgaged plantation would revert to the factor. Many *city* businessmen in New Orleans, owned plantations, scattered throughout the South, which they had gained this way.

*Right: The Carroll Manson, 1315 First, stands to the right of the Morris Mansion, 1331 First (other photo, following page)*

*Above: The Morris Mansion, 1331 First (story, previous page)*

The classically styled, double galleried house, at 1239 First, was built in 1857, by Albert Brevard. It acquired its side bays from its second owner, twelve years later. Much of the woodwork throughout the house is carved mahogany. The author, Anne Rice, now owns the house.

Across the street at 1236, is the home that John Gayle built for his bride in 1847. A much later house is at 2362 Camp. This Victorian, Queen Anne style home was designed by Architect Sully, for New Yorker Albert Ranlett, in 1889.

Judge Jacob Payne brought slaves from his upriver plantation to construct the, imposing mansion at 1134 First, in 1849. (Most of the Garden District houses were built with cheap immigrant labor – usually Irish – rather than valuable slave labor.)

Payne was from Kentucky, a prominent cotton factor, banker and speculator, in addition to his plantation and his judgeship. He acquired great debts during the War, when Union troops confiscated his property, and he never was able to recover, financially. His house was returned to him, later, and remained in his family until 1935.

"Spoons" Butler was one of the nicer names applied to the hated Union General Butler, when he was in charge of the Federal Occupation of New Orleans during the Civil War. Union officers, it seems, were delighted with the silverware, furnishings and grand homes of the prosperous defeated city, and freely helped themselves. Many confiscated homes were "refurnished" with belongings from several other houses. When Judge Payne's home was

*Magazine forms the unofficial dividing line between the Garden District and the "Irish Channel" (as the part of Lafayette City, that lay between Magazine and the River, became known). Here, the poorer, mostly Irish immigrants found work and housing along the crowded wharves*

*Above: The Brevard House, 1239 First*

*The thousands of flatboats, which brought goods down the Mississippi, riding the current, had no power for making a return trip. After unloading, they were broken up, and their heavy timbers were used in "paving" streets, or building many of the smaller homes of this area.*

returned to him, his neighbor's table stood in his dining room, but his own was never located.

Jefferson Davis, President of the Confederacy, was a close friend of Judge Payne. Davis often brought his family to stay in the Payne home on his visits to New Orleans. His daughter Winnie had her debut in this house. It was during one of these visits, in 1889, that Jefferson Davis died. Over 150,000 people paid their respects at City Hall (Gallier Hall) when his body lay in state there.

The Irish immigrants who came to the United States in the early 19th Century were among the very poorest, financially. In New Orleans, during those years, there were huge canals dug and other major building projects undertaken. Since the Irish were

plentiful and poor, they were the favored labor force. They were paid very little and had no protection as workers. If they were injured, killed or contracted yellow fever (as thousands did) they were easily replaced. There lives were worth very little in the booming city. African slaves had value. They had monetary value and they had to be fed, clothed and cared for, so, in general, they were seldom used for public works or jobs that involved dangerous conditions.

The Anderson Estate, at 2427 Camp, was originally a six pillared, double galleried house (similar to the Payne House down the block) when it was built for Hiram Anderson, in 1852. His fortune was made as a commission merchant. The house was rebuilt twice, entirely changing its design.

*The annual St. Patrick's Day Parade passes through the Irish Channel, and cabbages, potatoes and green trinkets are thrown to the crowds that line the parade route.*

*Above: An Italianate House, 1126 Second Right: The Adams House, 2423 Prytania*

property facing First Street. During the 1850's, she had the house moved to 1427 Second, and enlarged it from four to six columns in width.

John Adams (not the President) came from Ohio and proved successful as a wholesale grocer. In 1860, he constructed the striking cottage at 2423 Prytania. In modern years, workmen discovered a brick lined cellar, in the ground below where the cistern had once stood. Adams had built it for the storage of ice.

Joseph Maddox was editor of the "Daily Crescent" newspaper. In 1852, he built the handsome house at 2507 Prytania, putting in a "golden" ballroom, rich wood moldings and an Italian painted-tile fire place. A century later, the house was engulfed by fire, but rescued and carefully restored to near its original self.

At 2504 Prytania, the Women's Opera Guild uses their restored 1859 home for receptions and group tours. The ornate interior and period furniture give a glimpse back into the well to do life of 19th century, New Orleans. The octagonal tower was added later and now houses the "Salle de Souvenirs," displaying opera memorabilia.

New Yorker Henry Lonsdale arrived in 1828 and became successful supplying the gunny sacks used for the shipping of goods. Losing everything in the Panic of 1837, he left town. Returning as a coffee broker, he

At the corner of Camp and Second, a charming Victorian house shows a round, stained glass window. At 1126 and 1136 Second, there are two handsome Italianate homes. On the Second Street side of the Anderson House, an enormous tree and interesting service wing are visible.

A prominent Creole, Michel Musson, built two matching houses at 1229 and 1239 Second, for his sons, during the 1850's. One of them was owned later by Sarah Johnson, f.w.c. (which meant, "free woman of color"). Most of the free people of color, had their homes in the Creole parts of the city. Today, a large community of their descendants, live in some of those early neighborhoods, below Esplanade Avenue.

The 1850 house, at 2425 Coliseum, had the large Second Street section added later, and the galleries put all around. Much of the interior detail was restored, at that time.

Lewis Elkin made his fortune supplying the Oriental carpets, so popular during the flush Golden Era. His house, at 1410 Second, was designed as Greek Revival, and changed at the last minute, to include the Italianate features.

In 1844, Mrs. Amelia Fawcett built a Greek Revival home, on the back of her

prospered once again. Neighbors called him extravagant for spending so much on his striking home at 2521 Prytania, in 1857. Since the 1940's, his house has served as the Catholic Church for this neighborhood. Bald cypress trees, native to Louisiana, tower along the Third Street fence of the Lonsdale Home.

The Gothic Revival Cottage style was never very popular in New Orleans, being ill suited to the heat and humidity. But, an 1849 version of one, at 2605 Prytania, was adapted for the climate, somewhat, with the addition of the floor length windows and its gallery.

London born cotton broker, Thomas Gilmour, built the Italianate villa at 2520 Prytania, in 1853, for $9,500. (The price even included some silver plated hardware.) In recent years, a New Orleans historian restored the house to its original period.

The carriage house, at 1417 Third Street (of the Gilmour Villa on Prytania) was sold separately in about 1930. The subsequent owners added several rooms to the original carriage room (the broad doors on the right) and the harness room (on the left), creating a new home of substantial size.

The huge home at 1432 Third is a full century younger than most of its ornate neighbors. The exceptional quality of its materials and workmanship, and the addition of modern equipment, made it the

highest priced house in the Garden District, when it was constructed in 1961.

After Londoner Louis de Saulles bought the entire block of land at 2618 Coliseum (between Third, Fourth and Chestnut) he built his handsome home, in 1845. (photo, page 93) With the side of the building along Coliseum, its galleries faced the huge gardens in front and behind it. Widow Amenaide Fortin later owned the lone house, on its park like grounds. In 1878, to keep from losing the house to creditors, she divided and sold the rest of the block. The homes on either side, are actually in her front and back yards.

One of those homes, 2604 Coliseum, was constructed by James Mc Craken, when he bought the land from the Widow Fortin in 1878. He was born in Canada and had a furniture store on Royal Street. Indigo plants have grown for years, along the fence of the Mc Craken House. Indigo was an important crop in Louisiana's early years (used in making dye) before sugar cultivation became successful.

*Above: The Maddox House, 2507 Prytania*

89

# The Garden District

Walter Robinson came from Virginia, a successful cotton and tobacco dealer. He was quick to compound his wealth in banking, investments and real estate, and began his grand home at 1415 Third, in 1859. The elegance, inside and out, even extends to the unusual side carriage house. In recent times, the house has remained in the same family for more than fifty years.

Michel Musson was an exception – the lone Creole - building his home, at 1331 Third, in the middle of the "Americans." In 1850, he was President of the Cotton Exchange and Postmaster of the city. He was the uncle of French painter, Edgar Degas, who was often a guest in the house. The lacey cast iron galleries and Victorian style stables were added, in 1884.

The house at 1206 Third was built by wealthy planter, Bernard Kock, in 1852, as a classic, galleried home. When Confederate General John Hood bought the house, following the War, he made extensive changes to its appearance. He and his wife and one of their eleven children died of Yellow Fever, in 1878. The greenish flag stone in the sidewalk of the house was ordered by Kock from Europe. Since New Orleans has no natural stone, the flag stone and cobble stone, used in streets and sidewalks, was brought here as ballast, on the empty return trips of ships carrying goods to European markets.

Irish born Archibald Montgomery became wealthy in the post Civil War years, as President of the Crescent City Railroad. After the War, the railroads boomed, surpassing Steamboats as the major mode of transporting goods. When Montgomery built his home at 1213 Third, in 1867, architecture was beginning to vary from the popular classic styles.

A very *strong* variance from the popular styles is the Swiss Chalet, at 2627 Coliseum. A most unusual sight, in its semi tropical garden, the house was constructed for the daughter of Henry Buckner and her husband, James Eustis (Ambassador to France and a United States Senator). It was sold later, to the architect who had designed it, to be his home.

Another architect, William Freret, was well known in New Orleans, when he built a row of Garden District houses and sold

*Left: The Robinson Mansion, 1415 Third, (other photo, page 95) as seen through the lacey ironwork of the Musson House, 1331 Third*

# The Garden District

them. When beginning a similar row of five houses, at 2700 Coliseum, also for speculation, his construction and financing were interrupted by the Civil War. The buildings sat unfinished for several years, earning them the unfair nickname, Freret's Folly. The houses were originally identical.

The grand house at 1448 Fourth was built in 1859 for Colonel Henry Short, for $23,750. It has 16 foot ceilings and is surrounded by one of the two famous "corn stalk" fences (cast in Philadelphia). The Union Occupation saw Col. Short's villa chosen to be the headquarters for the new Governor. But the Commander of the Gulf "pulled rank," taking the house from the Governor for himself. Short's home was eventually returned to him, but his commission business had been ruined. He survived as a distiller, keeping the house until his death in 1890.

The builder brother of Mrs. Samuel Brown had begun construction of a house for her, at 1538 Fourth Street, in 1858, but was interrupted by the Civil War. In later years, a renovator of the house, removed the iron "lace" and some of the interior decor. Fortunately, it was found by the next owner, carefully packed away, and was then restored to the house.

The Rink, at 2727 Prytania, was a popular neighborhood skating rink, which opened in 1884, the year of the Great Cotton Centennial Exposition.

Across the street at 1500 Washington is the Southern Athletic Club. "Gentleman Jim" Corbett trained here, before winning the twenty one round fight with John L. Sullivan, in 1892.

Across Prytania, at 1423 Washington, is the arched entrance to Lafayette Cemetery #1. Many generations have been entombed here since 1833, when the City of Lafayette established this cemetery.

In 1880, Émile Commander opened his landmark restaurant, in the huge Victorian building at 1403 Washington. Famous for its fine Creole cuisine, Commander's Palace

*Below: The Montgomery House, 1213 Third (story, previous page)*

*Right: The "side" of the DeSaulles House, 2628 Coliseum*

*Right: The Short House, with its "cornstalk fence", 1448 Fourth*

*Lafayette Cemetery, opened in the heart of the Garden Districtin 1833, for the new city of Lafayette. The tombs were all put above ground, due to the water-saturated ground of the city. A visitor to New Orleans in those early years, observing the above ground tombs, often with little iron fences around them, and arranged in rows, along walkways, said that they looked like little cities, "Cities of the Dead."*

*Right: The "Seven Sisters", 2305-2329 Coliseum (story, page 74)*

has, for many years, been directed by members of the Brennan family.

On the corner, at 2731 Chestnut, is a small, Moorish style house. Shotgun houses were built throughout the city, making home ownership possible for poor working families, and inspiring an incredible creative diversity in decorative features and motifs.

In contrast to the small house, the entire 1200 block of Washington had been the garden of a great Italian "Renaissance Palazzo," built for James Robb, during the 1850's. Robb had begun as a West Virginia bank messenger at 13. By 32, he controlled New Orleans utility companies, as well as banks, railroads and other investments from San Francisco to New York. In 1855, he had filled his new mansion with expensive art, but by 1859, personal and financial disasters had caused him to sell it all. He left the city soon after.

Irish John Burnside was a successful dry goods merchant. During the early 1800's, he had bought Houmas House and nine other sugar plantations, earning himself the title of "Sugar King." Burnside bought the Robb Mansion to use as his "town house," and enjoyed the society of his wealthy Garden District neighbors until his death in 1881.

In 1890, the estate became campus of Newcomb College (now part of Tulane), and in 1918 it was home to The Baptist Theological Seminary. In 1955, the grand mansion was demolished for developers, with only some of the magnificent oaks, left standing.

In the next block, at 1126 Washington, the handsome house was built by the "Ice Man," A.W. Bosworth, who had come from Maine. It has been sadly in need of restoration for many years.

# The Garden District

When Newcomb College was using the Robb Villa as its campus (1890 to 1918) their art school flourished, adding its pottery department in 1897. They constructed their pottery building, at 2828 Camp Street, in 1902, and their unusual "Newcomb Pottery," soon earned international recognition and awards, during the early Twentieth Century.

At the next corner, 1240 Sixth Street was used as the Newcomb College School of Music. William Wright, cotton and commission merchant, had built the house in 1868. In 1953, after Newcomb had moved out, the building was completely restored to be a residence again. There is a "fire mark" on the front wall, used by the old fire companies to identify their insured.

The house at 2915 Chestnut was built for Dominique Stellar in 1867. Architects of the 19th Century often placed large, stately facades on more modest homes (as here) to evoke more feeling of grandeur. An unusual carriage house sits behind the main house.

John Peil bought the land for the raised cottage at 2912 Prytania, just before the Civil War. Grocery man Michael Hann built his pretty raised cottage nearby, at 2928, just after the War. His front gate is of an unusual Gothic style.

Attorney John Chilton died in 1859, the year that his house, at 1506 Seventh, was finished. The newspaper ad for selling the house boasted, "water works on the second floor." The flagstone walk is original.

The carriage house at 1512 Seventh, (for the next door house at 1506) was enlarged and converted into a residence in 1910. Henry Hansell's thriving saddle business provided the means for building his classical home at 3000 Prytania, in 1859.

During the 1850's, Architect Frederick Wing built the Greek Revival home at 1429 Seventh, to be his own home.

The house at 2925 Coliseum was built by Samuel Moore, who did a brisk business in crockery, china and glassware. The numerous and interesting modifications made over the years, to the rear service wing and the attic, are visible.

Just a block away from his own home, Architect Frederick Wing designed the impressive raised cottage at 1329 Seventh, for his grand daughters, in 1872. It had tennis courts and stables behind.

The two tall homes, at 1221 and 1215 Seventh, were built as identical wedding gifts for two sisters. They have each been modified quite differently since they were built, so now, there is little resemblance.

The author, George Washington Cable, was from Connecticut. He was enchanted with New Orleans and with the Garden District, especially. He built the raised cottage at 1313 Eighth, in 1874, and it soon became a meeting place for many other writers, including Mark Twain, Oscar Wilde and Joel Chandler Harris. Cable's books about life in New Orleans brought him recognition from the world, but disdain from the Creole community.

The Second Empire style house at 1437 Eighth was built facing Prytania. Daniel Byerly finished it in 1873. When the house was moved back and turned in 1927, the large rear service wing was demolished.

The style of the Victorian house at 3203 Prytania was chosen from an architectural catalogue which offered a variety of Queen Anne house styles and decor details to choose from.

The simple raised cottage at 1328 Harmony was being finished for John Chapman in April of 1862, when workmen on the roof spotted U.S. Navy ships on the River, carrying the Union forces who were arriving to occupy the city.

Thomas Pickles was a pharmacist, who bought a ferry boat. Eventually, he owned a fleet of ten ferries and grew prosperous enough to build the house at 3303 Coliseum, after the Civil War.

James Freret originally came from England. In New Orleans, he owned a cotton press and served a period as sheriff. He built the huge raised cottage at 1525 Louisiana, in 1852. His two sons became well known architects in the city.

The growing awareness of the value of the city's unusual architectural heritage, has achieved some measure of protection for these landmarks. Some houses have been lovingly maintained, throughout their years, often remaining in the same family for generations. But others have been rescued from demolition, or carefully restored after years of neglect and deterioration. It is not just the amazing *number* of historically valuable houses that have survived, but also, the completeness and character of so many entire neighborhoods, that makes the New Orleans heritage so unique.

*Above: The stately raised cottage, at 3116 Prytania, has an unusual dormer, which continues across the entire front roofline, providing a row of windows to the upper floor.*

*Above: Mark Twain on the front porch of the Cable Cottage, 1313 Eighth.*

*Left: The Robinson Mansion, 1415 Third (story, page 91)*

95

# Magazine Street

Beginning at Canal, Magazine Street is six miles of neighborhood shops and homes, with a character that changes every few blocks. In the first mile, it borders the Warehouse District, where much of the shipping and commerce used to be handled for the busy port.

At Magazine and Julia Street is a handsome 6 story building, which was constructed by Simon Hernsheim to be his cigar factory. Importing Cuban tobacco, he made cigars such as "La Belle Creole" and "Jackson Square." It was the largest cigar factory in the United States during the 1890's.

After passing under the ramps of the Mississippi River Bridge, Magazine runs just a few blocks from Coliseum Square, the first wealthy "American" neighborhood of the early 1800's.

When successful merchants in the crowded Faubourg St. Marie yearned for more tranquil surroundings, they planned the elaborate suburb called Coliseum Square. It was to be a center for the "revival of classical learning," with a coliseum for Olympic games, a prytanium (university), a carousel and a public forum. None of these were ever built, but many grand homes were.

Between Jackson and Louisiana, Magazine Street served as the bustling commercial business street that divided two communities - the grand area, known as the Garden District, and the Riverside neighborhood of smaller houses, known as the "Irish Channel" (named for the many Irish immigrants who settled along the riverfront, here).

*Right: A busy shop just off Magazine at the beginning of Prytania St. (now under the Mississippi River Bridge overpass). The delivery truck in front is from the Dixie Baking Company, at 3212 Magazine. Photo by Walker Evans, 1936, Farm Securities Administration*

*The Irish Channel still hosts a huge St. Patrick's Day Parade each year, when cabbages and green trinkets are tossed to the eager crowds who are all Irish, at least for the day.*

Today, Magazine is a kaleidoscope of interesting businesses - art galleries antique shops, boutiques, the studios of artists and artisans, coffee houses and bars, neighborhood restaurants, second hand galleries and snow ball stands - interspersed with homes. Store displays are of all types of collectables - contemporary and the myriad of treasures from the past. The variety of architectural styles and constant parade of people add to the unique character of this street.

At its far end, lies Audubon Park and Zoo, as the street runs close to the Mississippi River levee. The Zoo is one of the best in the country, with natural habitats and ecological exhibits.

*Above: Louisiana oysters are the specialty at Casamentos, which opened in 1919. The Half Moon Bar and Restaurant, at the 1900 block of Magazine*

*Many of the stores along Magazine were built with the shopkeepers' living quarters upstairs. Some of the charming homes along the street have become interesting shops and galleries.*

# Old Man River
## Life on the Mississippi keeps rolling along...

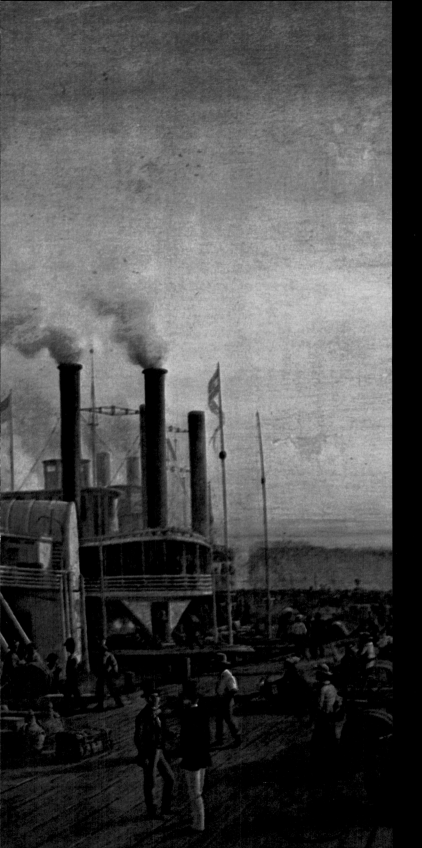

The Mississippi River was the reason for the existence of New Orleans. The early explorers from several nations realized the extreme value of the River, strategic, political and commercial, and they competed to protect the mouth of the River, in order to gain control of it. France was determined to build a colony to guard against the commercial and military interests of England and Spain. A strategic location was chosen for the French Colony on the River - land a little higher than the surrounding swamps, a little inland from the storms of the Gulf and a spot with a "back door" for emergency access to the Gulf (through the Lake).

Near the Canadian border, the River begins its 2,348 mile journey to the Gulf of Mexico, collecting all the combined waters of the Missouri and Ohio River Valleys in it's travels (over a million square miles from the Appalachian Mountains to the Rockies).

The River's yearly deposits of soil have built a vast delta of the rich farm land that made possible the great sugar and cotton plantations near New Orleans. The tremendous commercial traffic on the River during the 1800's all ended or began in New Orleans, creating wealth for the brokers, factors and shippers of the city. The River also connected most of America with the port of New Orleans. Ships from all over the world came to New Orleans through the Gulf, carrying products to be distributed up river and carrying the produce and manufacturing of the entire Mississippi Valley to foreign destinations. Along with this huge commercial exchange was the transportation of people as well. Wealthy foreign tourists, poor immigrants, adventurers, business men, plantation families (traveling to Europe or to their town houses in New Orleans, usually with their slaves) all used the River for transportation and were exposed to the ideas and cultures of the other passengers.

In the early years, the Colony built crude levees against the flooding of the River, but their main concern was in protecting the River itself from being taken by other foreign powers. Through the years, the designing and building of levee and spillway systems have been the challenging preoccupations. Now, we realize that the flood prevention problems, the vast and rich surrounding wet-lands (and all their related wildlife and sea life), the wealth from the petrochemical industry, the important commercial river barge traffic and the health of the River itself are all interrelated. The solutions we create have to include what is best for all of these aspects of living in peace with the Mississippi River.

*Left: "New Orleans Sugar Levee, by Henri Sebron, 1853, courtesy Louisiana State Museum*

*From 1800 to 1820, flat boats and keel boats plied the waters of the Mississippi carrying cargo on their arduous one way trips to New Orleans. The boats were then broken up for building or fire wood. The advent of steamboats, with the return trip under power and fully loaded, began the period of wealth on the River. By 1820, there were more than 60 steamboats on the Mississippi and by 1860, 1,000 of them were making round trips continually. Some were built just for cargo, but some were known as "floating palaces," of great splendor, with a variety of luxury for passengers.*

# Cities of the Dead

*Above: Old tombs in St. Louis Cemetery #3, on Esplanade*

*In St. Roch Cemetery near Elysian Fields, stands St. Roch Chapel. Built by a German American priest in thanks to St. Roch for sparing his congregation during the yellow fever epidemic of 1868, it has become a mecca for those in need of miracle cures.*

Parts of the city of New Orleans are actually below sea level, so the ground is saturated very close to the surface. In the early years there was constant flooding of the River, as well as the heavy rainfall. The first settlers had a problem with the burial of their dead, as the caskets would not stay below the ground. They soon began the system of above ground tombs and various styles of vaults. Cemeteries took on the appearance of miniature cities, with family tombs arranged in neat rows along walkways, many with little fences around them. They came to be called the "Cities of the Dead."

The outer walls of the cemeteries are formed of rows of attached vaults, stacked above each other. Often remains are moved to a lower chamber when a new casket is place above. Thus, a tomb can hold many generations of a family in a small space. Often, sections of vaults were bought by organizations that wished to offer an inexpensive burial plan to their members. Sometimes, a social or "mutual aid" club would actually build its own cemetery for its members (as with many of those around the

intersection of City Park Ave. and Canal).

The Church of the Dead stands at the corner of Rampart and Conti. Père Antoine laid the corner stone in 1826, to begin a new burial chapel for the cemeteries nearby. It had been decided that it was not safe to hold funerals in the St. Louis Cathedral any more, for fear of contagion from yellow fever and other plagues.

St. Louis Cemetery #1 has most of the oldest tombs in the City. It was opened just outside the ramparts of the Vieux Carré, in 1788, on what is now Basin Street. Among the many famous people buried here are mayors of New Orleans and Marie Laveau (the Voodoo Queen - whose grave is still marked with X's for good luck).

St. Louis Cemetery # 2 opened in 1823, when #1 had become filled. The annual epidemics of yellow fever and other deadly diseases filled up the cemetery with large numbers of dead at a time. (They also caused New Orleans to have an unusually high number of orphans, and of groups dedicated to their care and protection.) St. Louis #2 covers three blocks, behind the present housing project on St. Louis.

*Right: In a New Orleans cemetery – a wall of burial vaults (often referred to as "ovens")*

*The statue of Saint Expedite stands in the chapel of the Church of the Dead. Long ago, a crate was delivered to the church. It bore no name or place of origin, just the word, "Expedite." Inside was a statue, so it became known as Saint Expedite*

Lafayette Cemetery #1, in the Garden District, at 1423 Washington, opened in 1833, as the American's answer to the older Creole cemeteries.

St. Louis Cemetery # 3 is in the 3300 block of Esplanade. Many notable residents have been entombed behind its beautiful gates, since 1854.

There are at least 14 old cemeteries, grouped together at the intersection of City Park Avenue and Canal, which are all newer than the ones discussed previously. But, they too, offer a fascinating visit into New Orleans' history, and contain some of the more spectacular styles of tombs in the city.

The Day of the Dead (All Saints' Day) is November First, and has been celebrated in New Orleans since the early years. Families visit the cemeteries in the last days of October, to clean and white wash the graves and pull weeds. Stone cutters are often busy getting new plaques made. On the first, families gather in the cemeteries, with flowers for the graves and prayers and with best wishes for other families and relatives. There are religious ceremonies and respects are paid to graves of friends and relatives.

On All Saints' Day, tombs used to be draped in flags or black, before flowers and candles were arranged on them. Orphans would stand at the gates of the cemeteries to receive donations. By night fall, many thousands of bouquets would have been placed in the cemeteries

Another tradition in New Orleans cemeteries is the use of what are known as "everlasting flowers." Instead of fresh flowers, which last only a few days, these are made of metal and glass, and keep their decorative vigil all year, through rain and sun.

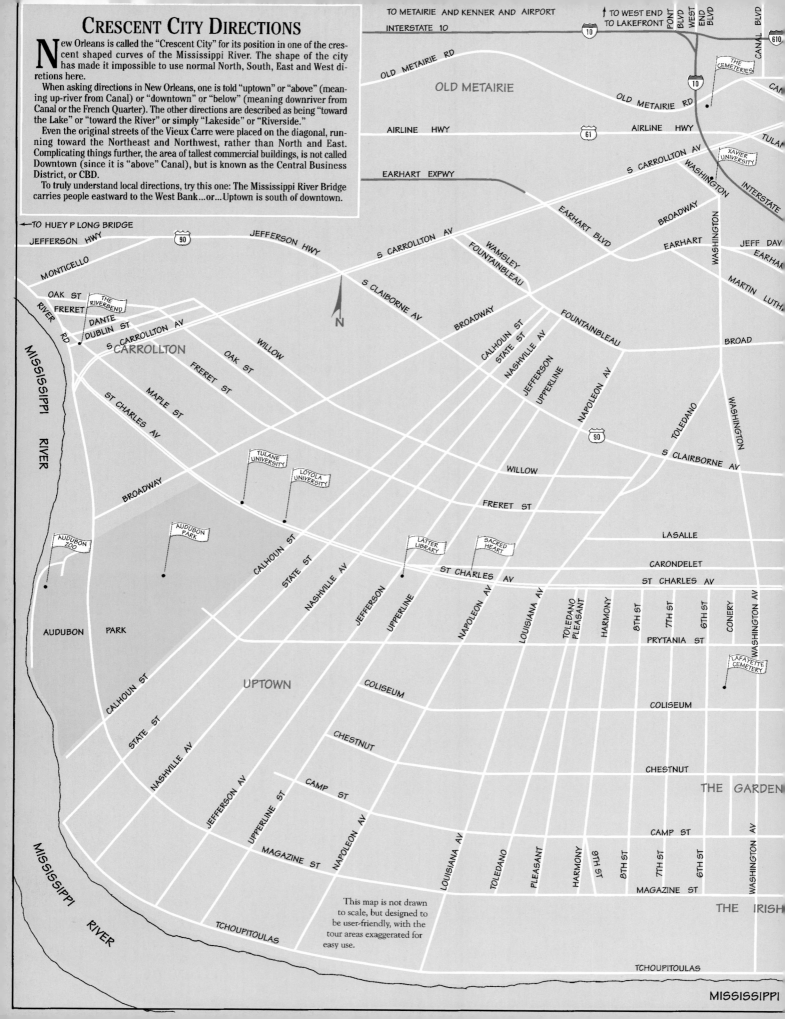

# CRESCENT CITY DIRECTIONS

New Orleans is called the "Crescent City" for its position in one of the crescent shaped curves of the Mississippi River. The shape of the city has made it impossible to use normal North, South, East and West directions here.

When asking directions in New Orleans, one is told "uptown" or "above" (meaning up-river from Canal) or "downtown" or "below" (meaning downriver from Canal or the French Quarter). The other directions are described as being "toward the Lake" or "toward the River" or simply "Lakeside" or "Riverside."

Even the original streets of the Vieux Carre were placed on the diagonal, running toward the Northeast and Northwest, rather than North and East. Complicating things further, the area of tallest commercial buildings, is not called Downtown (since it is "above" Canal), but is known as the Central Business District, or CBD.

To truly understand local directions, try this one: The Mississippi River Bridge carries people eastward to the West Bank...or...Uptown is south of downtown.

This map is not drawn to scale, but designed to be user-friendly, with the tour areas exaggerated for easy use.

# Esplanade, the Bayou and the Lakefront

## Les Bon Temps Roulez

### Gambling and Dueling were among the passions of the Creoles

Esplanade became the Grand Avenue of the Creole part of the city, their aristocratic residential street. In the 1830's to 1850's, as wealthy Creole families living in the old French Vieux Carré began moving to new homes along the "lower" edge of the old Quarter (farther away from the Americans), the early Creole cottages on Esplanade, were gradually replaced by grander townhouses.

At 741 Esplanade, stands a home that was designed for Adrien Barbey in 1859. Its gabled chimneys and cast iron galleries are typical of Creole townhouses. Achille Murat, nephew of Napoleon, lived for two years in the house at 917 Esplanade, before losing it to creditors in the Panic of 1837.

The famous Creole, Bernard de Marigny, had his grand home and plantation just below Esplanade through the early 1800's. A flamboyant and very wealthy *bon vivant*, from an old, prominent and well respected Creole family, he heartily indulged in excesses of many kinds. Gambling in any form was his favorite addiction, and he was known to sometimes loose thousands of dollars to one roll of the dice. But he also fought 19 duels, drank and dined to excess,

womanized, gave extravagant banquets, lavishly entertained many of the notable visitors to the city and bought luxurious furnishings, paintings and even land, without asking the price.

Marigny was responsible for introducing the game of Craps to New Orleans (having learned it from visiting French royalty in 1798) and he lost much of his fortune to the game. In 1805, when his excessive debts forced him to subdivide and sell part of his estate, he named one of the streets of his new Faubourg, *Rue de Craps*, in honor of his losses. The street name was later changed to *Burgundy*, when a Methodist church was built and members objected to people calling it the *Craps Methodist Church*.

This section down river from Esplanade is still called "Faubourg Marigny" after this "bigger than life" Creole. It has retained many of the other street names he created, including *Desire*, (thus the famous streetcar) *Goodchildren*, *Piety* and *Love*. In modern times, as costs of living in the French Quarter have gone up, much of the artistic and Bohemian community has moved across Esplanade to the Faubourg. Music, art and good food are flourishing there.

Above: "A Fencing Lesson," Harper's Magazine, 1887 Most New Orleans gentlemen took classes with one of the colorful and chivalrous "fencing masters" There were about 50 salons, mostly in Exchange Alley. The fencing masters were revered like modern sports heroes and many became wealthy from so many students.

The mansion at 1020 Esplanade was built for William Nott in 1835. Political boss, John Slidell bought it in 1851, to give as a wedding present to his wife's sister, upon her marriage to Gen. P.T. Beauregard, ("The Great Creole" of later Civil War fame). Then, during the period of intense Italian immigration to New Orleans, The Unione Italiana, a "social and mutual aid" society, bought the house in 1912. An Italian facade and a dance hall were added.

Looking forgotten, at the hectic intersection with Claiborne, 1519 Esplanade had been the pride of Mrs. Eliza Marsoudet. She specified every detail of its construction in 1846, including the upstairs ballroom (which was well used for many years).

A prominent Creole attorney, Cyprien Dufour, built the Italianate style mansion at 1707 Esplanade in 1859. It was his third home on the Avenue.

Michel Musson, the Creole uncle of French impressionist painter Edgar Degas, owned the house at 2306 Esplanade, before

he moved to the Garden District.

At 2453 Esplanade is the survivor of a pair of twin houses, with Mansard roofs, built for manufacturer George Washington Dunbar and his children in 1873.

Florence Luling had built a home in the Garden District, before the Civil War. Then, making a fortune in war time commerce, he returned to New Orleans after the war and built the massive villa in the 3300 block of Esplanade. The enormous house stands on the remaining ten acres of his eighty acre estate. In 1871, he sold the villa to be the Jockey Club for the Fairgrounds Racetrack, which lies directly behind it. (photo page 106)

The Fairgrounds Racetrack is the third oldest operating horse track in the United States, opening its doors in 1872. (There had been organized racing in the city since 1804 and later, there were four popular tracks in operation at once.) New Orleans has always been a gambling town, and horse racing somewhat replaced the popularity of

The old oaks along the edge of City Park were known as the Dueling Oaks, and were a popular spot, out side the city for "affairs of honor." Though Dueling was forbidden by both Church and Law, many of the highest officials could be found under the Oaks. Until the Civil War, there was hardly a man in public life who had not fought at least one duel.

Claiborne, the first American Governor of Louisiana, fought a duel with Daniel Clark, a Member of Congress. Emile LaSere, U.S. Representative from Louisiana, fought eighteen duels during his career. George Waggaman, US Senator from Louisiana, was killed in a duel, in 1843, by Dennis Prieur, former Mayor of New Orleans.

betting on cock fights, bull fights and bloody matches between bulls and bears. It is still a very popular betting sport here.

Next to the Jockey Club, is the entrance to St. Louis Cemetery #3. Many former residents of Esplanade are entombed in its rows of vaults.

Esplanade ends at Bayou St. John facing City Park and the entrance leading to the New Orleans Museum of Art. This nationally recognized museum was begun in 1911, with the extensive collection of prominent citizen, Isaac Delgado. The grand statue is of revered Creole hero of the Confederacy, General Pierre Gustave Toutant Beauregard.

City Park was the sugar plantation of a Creole gentleman, Louis Allard, in the late 1700's. More poet than business man, he lost his land to John McDonogh, (father of New Orleans public schools) who allowed him to still live there. When McDonogh died, he left the 1,500 acres of wooded land and lagoons to the City of New Orleans.

Many park features were built by the WPA during the 1930's and there is an old and colorful; working carousel. The park has facilities for a variety of recreational activities and has always been popular for family outings.

In the park are the famous Dueling Oaks. These venerable old trees were standing here, on the Allard Plantation, far enough away from the authorities of the 1700's and early 1800's, to be a good setting for proud New Orleanians to settle their "affairs of honor." Beneath their gnarled branches, "seconds" observed strict protocol for the duels, using a variety of weapons and the slightest of grievances. Many a tombstone in the cemetery nearby,

The neighborhood between Esplanade and Elysian Fields is known as the Seventh Ward. Many of the descendants of the "free persons of color" live in this area, sharing a somewhat separate and unique cultural heritage, with strong emphasis on education, the arts, tradition and family.

Left: The Spanish Customs House, 1342 Moss, on Bayou St. John

109

reads, "Lost on the field of honor."

At the end of Esplanade, just before the entrance to City Park, is a small street called Moss Ave, which runs along the banks of Bayou St. John. The Bayou was one of the reasons that Bienville established New Orleans where he did. Boats could be brought in from the Gulf, through Lake Pontchartrain and down the Bayou - a sort of back door to the city - leaving only a short walk along the old Indian path to the town. In 1805 a canal was dug from Bayou St. John, ending in a basin (Basin Street) where boats could be docked and unloaded at the edge of the city. In 1938, the basin and canal were filled in.

During the early years, Bayou St. John was lined with plantation houses, their crop lands stretching out to the east and west of the little waterway. Though the lands of these plantations were all subdivided and sold in the second half of the 1800's, many of the old plantation houses are still in use.

The Pitot House is at 1440 Moss. This West Indies style house, built in 1799, was bought in 1810 as a "country house" by the then Mayor, James Pitot. (It has been open for touring.) A French aristocrat, Jacques Pitot de Beaujardiere had fled the guillotine in France by going to live in French Santo Domingo. Escaping the 1791 slave uprising there, he made his way to New Orleans and prospered as a prominent civic and business leader. Adopting American democratic ideals, he became, simply, James Pitot when he was appointed as the first *American* mayor of the city in 1805.

The Blanc House, at 1342 Moss was built in about 1834, for Evariste Blanc. It is now the rectory for the Church directly behind it (photo page 107).

The house at 1300 Moss has been called by many names, including the "Spanish Customs House". A West Indies style plantation house, it was built for Captain Elie Beauregard, in 1784.

A high class gambling salon was opened along Bayou St. John, as a luxurious hide away for wealthy gamblers. It was the second gambling enterprise opened by John Davis, another educated and cultured émigré from Santo Domingo. His gambling house in the Vieux Carré provided luxurious decor, classical music, art and fine food and drink to his patrons. His "salons" were in sharp contrast to the rowdy and lawless "joints" all over the city, where fighting, murder and shanghais were often the common fare.

Davis had opened New Orleans' first theater in the Vieux Carré, providing the city with excellent and very well attended drama, opera and ballet. His gambling salons were very popular with the wealthy Creoles, including Bernard de Marigny and his friends. Thousands of dollars (as well as homes and plantations) were won and lost each evening at Davis' fancy gaming tables.

Soon a new type of gambler appeared in the game rooms of New Orleans, with the advent of steamboats on the Mississippi. These sharp witted characters ranged from well mannered, sporting "gentlemen," (possibly cultured and "honorable") to cheats looking for a "mark" or a fight. They "worked" on the "floating palaces" up and down the River, but often spent time at the tables in New Orleans (both in high class salons and common rowdy joints).

Returning on Moss again, to where it meets Esplanade, leave the intersection on City Park Ave, a short street which borders the park between Esplanade and the cluster of the many cemeteries near the inter-section with Canal Blvd..

At 900 City Park Ave. is the Tavern on the Park. Frenchman Jean Marie Saux opened his coffee house here in 1860, across from the Dueling Oaks. Later, it became a tavern, popular with the patrons and Madames of Storyville (the famous red-light district near the French Quarter). Subsequent owners attracted customers with a speak easy and a back room for gambling, before the tavern was made a restaurant once again.

At Canal Blvd. turn right. Then a left on either Harrison Ave. or Robert E. Lee will take you over to Pontchartrain Blvd., the main road going to West End and the lake.

Lake Pontchartrain is about 40 miles long and 25 miles wide - its width crossed (in Metairie) by the Pontchartrain Cause-way, one of the longest bridges in the world. The Lake is unusual, in that its relatively shallow waters are brackish - a natural mixture of salt and fresh waters.

Just to the west of West End is the neighborhood called Bucktown, a cluster of homes, restaurants (mostly seafood) and the docks for its small fleet of commercial fishing boats. During Prohibition times, speakeasies and rough gambling spots were popular here (just over the Parish line from city officials). Many New Orleanians con-tinued their usual traditions of gambling in various forms, while all related varieties of vice continued to thrive, as well. Authorities were either paid off or were openly corrupt participants in illegal activities.

New Orleans was so accepting of gambling that during Prohibition, many Church bazaars or school festivals would borrow the illegal gambling machines for the day from a neighborhood speak easy or bar, as part of the open entertainment and fund raising for their family events.

During the 1800's, gambling houses were legally licensed one year and outlawed the next, as ambivalent law makers devised

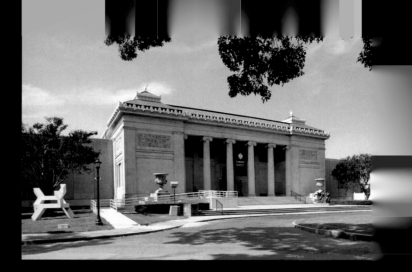

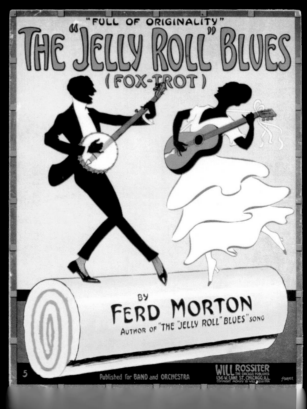

Top: T
Museu
in City
Openec

Above:
carouse
an ente
from a

Left: T
cover fo
"Jelly F
written
New C
Jazz m
and co
Ferdin
"Jelly F
Morton

new plans for controlling vice. During the 1880's, corruption and illegal activities were flourishing. Desperate City fathers voted in a plan to curb vice - "gambling, prostitution and female sensational dancing" were restricted to "districts," where they could be controlled, (even though still illegal).

Instead of curbing or controlling these activities, Storyville (the popular district) became a famous attraction, that locals frequented and visitors didn't miss. It was then completely shut down in 1917.

During the 1800's, the resort-recreation destinations of West End, Spanish Fort and Milneburg developed along the lake shore. Crowds from the city flocked to the casinos, restaurants, night clubs, hotels, amusement parks, theaters and pavilions. Some families just enjoyed the gardens, picnic grounds or bath houses and swam or fished and crabbed along the water's edge.

*Above: New Orleans is blessed with a variety and abundance of excellent seafood from all the surrounding waters. Dining at the Lakefront has been popular since the city's early years.*

*Left: A view of water games at West End, celebrating French Bastille Day, July 14, 1881*

*Right: Boats tied along Bayou St. John about 1910*

Folks came to the Lake by a mule drawn street car (later electrified) which rumbled along Pontchatrain Blvd. to West End, or by a rail road line, *Smokey Mary,* opened in 1831, which puffed along Elysian Fields to Milneburg. Spanish Fort was between the two, at the mouth of Bayou St. John. These festive recreation areas thrived well into the first decades of the 1900's. Many early Jazz musicians developed their styles, playing in the band concerts and night club shows here.

Founded in 1849, the Southern Yacht Club built a large sailboat harbor and ornate clubhouse at West End in 1879. Their regattas and races entertained the crowds along the shore. Orleans Marina was built next to the yacht harbor, as power boats gained in popularity. West End is still the city's busy boating center.

Along the shore, hundreds of "camps" were built at the end of long narrow piers, extending far out over the water. These unusual structures were used by city families as summer or weekend homes. Perched on pilings, they ranged from large cottages, complete with screened porches, to tiny tin roofed fishing shacks.

During the 1930's, a "stepped" seawall, Lake Shore Drive and a long park were built from West End to the

Industrial Canal, giving the public good access to the shoreline for swimming, fishing, picnics, sports and the beautiful view. The ornate resort buildings and the "camps" were lost to this modern design of the lake shore.

A new recreation destination was built called Pontchartrain Beach Amusement Park. It entertained throngs of *white* New Orleanians from 1928 until its closing in 1983. Nearby, and later, a smaller area for entertainment and recreation for black New Orleanians was constructed. It flourished from 1954 to 1964.

Through most of the city's history, families enjoyed Lake Pontchartrain for swimming and boating, as well as catching crabs, shrimp and a variety of fish. But by 1970, it was well on its way to becoming a dead lake due to commercial dredging. (The dredging residue covered the lake's water plants, which aerate the water and provide food and nurseies to the many species of water creatures.) A small group of citizens fought long and hard to save the Lake, with education and court battles. Uniting, New Oleanians did save their lake and it is on its way to being clear and teeming with life once more. Now the huge job of saving the surrounding wetlands is the important focus for the future.

# Jean Laffite and The Battle of New Orleans
## The Pirate Offered $5,000 for the Capture of the Governor !

*Above: Paintings of the Battle of New Orleans, courtesy The Historic New Orleans Collection, "Pirate" Jean Laffite, smuggler, privateer and patriot*

When Jean Laffite and his brothers first appeared in New Orleans, around 1805, their name was not yet notorious. They were just Frenchmen from the West Indies. Pierre opened a small blacksmith shop on Bourbon and Jean began selling imported goods, fabrics, spices and household items.

For many years, a group of smugglers, known as the Baratarians, had been operating from the network of bayous and swamps around Barataria Bay, about 60 miles south of the city, off the Gulf of Mexico. In 1807, when the law was passed, prohibiting further importation of slaves into the United States, slave *smuggling* became a very profitable business. African slaves (black gold, as they were called) were bought from privateers, who stole them from slave ships at sea. The privateers also sold the Baratarians a variety of merchandise, similarly stolen from merchant ships.

Jean Laffite soon became the middle man, between the Baratarian smugglers and the merchants of New Orleans. Within two years, he had become a major slave trader, and a rich and powerful man, admired by many. With prosperous business men and lawyers among his friends, he quickly grew so disdainful of American law, that he openly held public auctions of slaves and merchandise. These advertised sales, held near Barataria, became gala events, with excursion boats bringing even high society ladies and gentlemen for entertaining afternoons of illegal "shopping."

Governor Claiborne became increasingly agitated at the impunity with which Laffite carried on his business, and the fact that the local population, especially the Creoles, seemed to be on the outlaw's side. Late in 1812, the Governor's forces ambushed the Laffites and a group of Baratarians. When

*A "Free Jack" was a slave, who, in return for his help in the Battle of New Orleans, was granted freedom by Andrew Jackson. The only legible words on the documents issued to these men, were "free" and part of the General's signature. Some people still say that they are descended from a "Free Jack."*

the Laffites failed to appear for trial and their confiscated goods mysteriously vanished from government warehouses, the enraged Claiborne posted a $500 reward for the capture of Jean Laffite, "that hooligan"! In a short time, a notice from Laffite was seen posted in the Vieux Carré, offering a $5,000 reward for the capture of the Governor!

Just as Creole Louisiana became the eighteenth state in the Union, the U.S. went to war with England again – the War of 1812. The war dragged on until Napoleon was defeated in 1814. England then turned all of its effort against the United States. Governor Claiborne was concerned that the Baratarians' large fleet of ships might fall into British hands, if they tried to take New Orleans and gain control of the mouth of the Mississippi. He resolved to destroy the pirates' stronghold.

At the same time, the British arrived near Barataria Bay to make a proposition to Laffite. They offered him rank, money, protection and amnesty, for him and his men, in exchange for his help against the

Americans. He stalled them, politely, while sending his own proposal (along with the British offer) to the Americans. He offered his men and his large stores of ammunition and supplies, in return for pardons for himself and his men. Claiborne ignored his offer and sent troops to attack the pirate settlement. They burned a few ships, confiscated nine, loaded with expensive merchandise, and jailed some of the smugglers.

When Gen. Andrew Jackson arrived in the city in December of 1814, to prepare a defense, he thought the situation was hopeless. With no fortifications, an untrained and motley group of citizens-soldiers and no supplies or ammunition, he believed the British would easily take the city. There are many stories as to how and where Jackson and Laffite met, but Jackson quickly accepted Laffite's offer of help, and together, they planned a strategy of defense for the city. (Even after Claiborne's raid, Laffite still had great stores of ammunition, which the Americans desperately needed.) The brave little army that Jackson organized

included Creoles, "Free Men of Color," slaves, Germans, Acadians, Americans and Indians, in addition to the regulars and militia men Jackson had brought from Kentucky. The jailed smugglers were released, and 1,500 Baratarians were put under the command of Dominique You (a Laffite brother). This little make-shift army was to face 12,000 British troops, well equipped and well trained.

After days of skirmishes, the Battle of New Orleans took place on Jan. 8, 1815. The Americans opened artillery fire on the rows of advancing "red coats," who marched in measured time. They followed with fire from their crack shot rifles. The short and bloody battle left 2,000 British casualties with only a handful of "Americans" dead. But, ironically, the battle should have never taken place. The Treaty of Ghent, ending the war, had been signed two weeks before, but the news of its signing had not yet reached New Orleans.

Each January, a reenactment of the famous battle, is held on the battleground at Chalmette National Historical Park.

# Plantation Life of Southern Louisiana

**The wealth of New Orleans, before the Civil War, was inseparable from that of the great sugar plantations, which stretched along the river nearby.**

*Left: The Garçonnière of Houmas House Plantation (quarters for bachelor sons or gentlemen visitors)*

In the mid 1700's, while New Orleans was still just a colonial outpost, great tracts of land, on both sides of the Mississippi were issued to wealthy Frenchmen. Some of the large ones, close to the city, stretched from the river to the lake. All of these tracts were long and thin, arranged like segments of a fan along the curves of the Mississippi, so that each could have a piece of riverfront, however narrow, for transportation of its goods and people. Most of the great plantation houses were built close to the river, with the fields of crops stretching back from the house.

The swampy land was thick with cypress, mosquitoes, heat and humidity. Clearing for planting was difficult, but the soil was rich and the cypress had value, when sold in New Orleans. The biggest problem was the same for the plantations, as for the city — a constant war had to be waged against the flooding river. Levees were built and canals dug, to drain and irrigate, but the flooding caused continual loss of crops and property.

The early plantations grew indigo for export (used in making dye). Cotton, tobacco, rice, fruits and vegetables were also cultivated, but for local consumption.

Even in this difficult frontier setting, the illusions of grandeur these French gentlemen possessed, filled frontier homes with luxury furnishings and imported decor, and inspired the planting of "alleys" of oaks along their entrance roads from the river. Sometimes their original cottages were replaced with impressive mansions. But the South of legend - the idealized plantation life - was to bloom, not with these early indigo plantations, but in the 1800's, when sugar became the fortune making crop of this section of the Mississippi.

During the 1790's, an epidemic of worms, coupled with declining prices, brought indigo production to halt. Planters were desperate to find a new crop for export. Sugar was creating great wealth in the West Indies, but all attempts to granulate it, in Louisiana, had failed.

*Above: Houmas House, built in 1840, for The Prestons, daughter and son in law of Gen. Wade Hampton, who had begun the famous sugar plantation in 1812. He had cabins for 500 slaves. It later belonged to John Burnsides, "the sugar king," who expanded the plantation to 20.000 acres.*

*Above: An elegant bedroom at Houmas House Plantation*

*Above: "Along the River Road" (an old Currier and Ives print) Most of the sugar plantations near New Orleans, had their houses near the River*

Finally, in 1795, a courageous and aristocratic Creole planter, Étienne de Boré, staked the last of his fortune on a sugar crop, on his plantation near the city (the present day Audubon Park). He invested in granulating equipment and an "expert" from the West Indies. To the joy of his fellow planters, the experiment was a success, and soon, everyone had replanted in sugar cane, creating the new industry that was to help make New Orleans so wealthy.

While the rest of the deep South grew cotton (much of which came through the port of New Orleans), southeast Louisiana built massive fortunes on the production of sugar and molasses.

Starting a sugar crop, took tremendous capital. Pieces of cane were buried in irrigated furrows in early spring. By late summer, the new cane was taller than a man. But, to develop fully, it had to grow as long into fall as possible. An early frost or bad flood could wipe out an entire year's crop.

It took strong adults to cut the cane, and during the month of cutting, slaves worked 18 hours a day, or in round the clock shifts. The cut cane was then carried on carts to the sugar mill (usually on the plantation). The mill, run either by a steam engine or horses, pressed the juice from the stalks. This liquid was then boiled in huge open kettles, until the exact moment for granulation. Syrup which didn't granulate, was then saved as molasses. The kettles had to be watched continually.

The fuel for boiling the kettles was one of the largest expenses. In 1843, Norbert Rillieux, a black man, invented a process of boiling the cane juice in vacuum pans, to retain the vapor for heating other pans. This process cut fuel cost tremendously.

If a sugar plantation was successful, the owner could live a life of luxury, wealth and grandeur. Diaries and other records tell of parties, masquerade balls and banquets. Planters amused themselves with hunting or fishing expeditions, gambling, duels, racing horses, reading, strolls through their beautiful gardens or long conversations over mint juleps or cigars — very much like the movies portray.

One of the favorite activities of plantation families seems to have been "visiting." An entire family (with servants) would travel to visit another, staying from a

few days to a month or more. Plantation households graciously accommodated such visitors, extending every hospitality, and expected the same when they went visiting. Sometimes these excursions were to the homes of friends or relatives in New Orleans, and many of the planters bought town houses in the city, for regular stays.

Not everyone near New Orleans was wealthy like the sugar planters. There were hard working farmers who lived in simple frontier houses and struggled all their lives with the hardships of climate and flood.

But, sugar plantation mansions were built with increasing luxury, as neighbors competed to impress each other. Most were built near the riverbank, with a grand entrance leading to the two story, high roofed house, with pillars to support the galleries (sometimes on all four sides).

The "big house" was surrounded by many smaller buildings: garçoniéres (separate quarters for bachelor sons or visiting business men), pigeoniers (for pigeons and doves), kitchens, store houses and the big sugar houses. Behind were rows of slave cabins, the slave hospital, the overseer's house and then, finally, the fields.

In these homes, it was not unusual to feed and entertain fifty guests for an evening. Planters prided themselves on the amount and variety of wild game they placed on their tables. (Most had a slave who served as a full time hunter.) New Orleanians cherished their invitations to plantation dinners.

Meals were long and leisurely, with an amazing number of courses. One plantation house had a miniature railroad, which carried the huge steaming dishes of food to the table. Often, wealthy planters hired famous chefs to prepare their special dinner parties with themes.

Every plantation had a boat dock and a few boats. There were fishing boats, work boats (for carrying lumber and sugar to market, or bringing back supplies and purchases) and family boats (for taking every one to Sunday Mass, for visiting neighbors or for taking a shopping holiday in New Orleans).

Sir Walter Scott had a great influence on the Louisiana sugar planters of the 1800's. Chivalry pervaded every aspect of life and each plantation had a romantic name, many taken from Scott novels.

But the idyllic life of these prosperous planters was always under the heavy shadow of slavery, ironically, the very basis of its wealth and leisure. As in records of slavery elsewhere in the South, there were both caring and cruel masters, tolerable and frightful conditions, opportunities with hope and misery with no hope. But no master could escape the constant presence of the contradictions inherent in owning other people, however it might be justified by religion, greed, philosophy, science, politics, might or need.

From the earliest years of the colony, slavery in Louisiana was controlled by the "Code Noir" (Black Code). The Code set forth rules for both slave and master. Slaves had to be provided with "adequate" housing, clothing and minimum standards of corn and pork. There were limits on the number of lashes a slave could receive in one day. They had to work from sunup to sundown, with a lunch break (two hours on the long hot days of summer). They could not be made to work on Holy Days, Christmas week or Sundays, without being paid. (Most had all or part of Saturdays off, too.)

Household slaves were usually better off than those who worked the cane fields. They often wore livery or the family's hand me down clothes. They ate much of the same food as the planter and were allowed more dignity and privileges.

Planters' children usually had slave companions, who slept at the foot of their beds, played with them and grew up to be their personal servants. "Mammies" often breastfed the white babies and were given most of the responsibility for raising the children. They usually commanded respect from both children and parents.

Often, house slaves learned skills such as horse training, gardening or carpentry, making them invaluable to their masters. Some were trusted to go to other plantations or to New Orleans to conduct business or take messages for the master, often with fancy clothes and flowery manners.

*Left: The kitchen at Houmas House Plantation, authentically restored to the period before 1840.*

Field slaves lived in rows of crude cabins behind the big house. They were given the simplest of clothing, shoes and furniture. They worked under an overseer, who was usually responsible for their discipline. For offenses ranging from the "wrong attitude" or "laziness," to lying, stealing or running away, the most common punishment was whipping. But there were iron collars, the withholding of food or privileges or the cutting of an arm or leg, to permanently scar or deform.

Most field slaves had chickens, pigs and gardens, which they cared for at night and on the weekends. They usually could eat what they raised and could sell any extra eggs or vegetables for spending money. A few masters allowed them to save toward buying their freedom, but usually their money was to be spent for special clothes for Sunday church.

Many planters gave parties for their slaves on holidays or for slave weddings, providing hams or turkeys and whiskey for the meal and dance. Special food, whiskey and money were given to slaves for Christmas and the Christmas week of holidays.

Probably the heaviest burden of slavery placed on the planters was the constant fear of their own slaves. The "Code Noir" made it a severe offense to sell whiskey or fire arms to slaves or to allow slaves from different plantations to congregate. Slaves were forbidden to testify against white men in court. The worst dread for the slave, was that of the slave auction – the possibility of a slave being permanently separated from his family.

Slaves had value and their health was a concern to planters. There was always a slave "hospital" and a doctor was usually paid a set fee, per slave, per year, to keep them healthy. Pregnant or nursing mothers were seldom given hard work or punishment, to protect the health of baby and mother. Most slaves were kept from dangerous jobs, which were given instead to white Irish immigrants.

The continual prosperity of many of the plantations was helped by a system of self sufficiency. They exported their large production of sugar and molasses, and some times other crops, for their main financial profit. As well, the produce from their large gardens, and the milk, eggs and butter, were all eagerly bought by the city markets. But their need to import to the plantation (except for luxury items) was very small. Most of the necessities for the large extended household (which included family members, overseers' families and all the slaves) were produced on the land.

Many plantations raised their own sheep for wool. An abundance of geese, ducks, turkeys, and chickens were kept for eggs and cooking. A herd of cattle provided meat and all of the dairy products needed. Corn, rice and hay were cultivated, to be used for household needs and to feed the livestock. Hogs were raised by both slaves and planters. The river provided fish and shellfish, while game birds and small woods animals augmented the standard table fare. Behind the legendary gardens of fragrant flowers, lay orchards of fruit and pecans.

Plantations took pride in their stables of horses for riding, and for their carriages, and they also raised mules for working. Among the slaves on the de Boré plantation, there were such skilled craftsmen as masons, carpenters, a blacksmith, wheel wrights, horse trainers, seamstresses and a shoe maker. Slaves gathered driftwood from the river, to be used for firewood and cut cypress to sell to the city.

On Étienne de Boré's plantation (like most) slaves were summoned each morning by a large bell. Once gathered, de Boré, or another family member, would lead the assembly in prayer, before giving the day's instructions. The bell would call them again at dusk for evening prayers before dismissal for the day.

John McDonogh, (who paid for most of New Orleans' early public schools) had a sugar plantation across the River in what is now Gretna. He owned 300 slaves (a large number) during the 1840's. Regarded as crazy by his neighbors, he believed that the low productivity of slavery was the result of low morale. He insisted that slaves could develop industry, good will, latent abilities and "more intelligence" if given incentive and hope. He gave his slaves opportunities

*Above right: Mint Juleps are a traditional Southern drink made with bourbon, sugar, and mint leaves.*

*Right: Once centers of bustling activity many plantation houses offer modern visitors a picturesque, tranquil setting.*

to earn and save money toward buying their freedom. He created a jury system among his slaves for the handling of discipline. Visitors reported his slaves to be cheerful, industrious and devoted. Many learned good vocational skills, two went to college in the North and several bought their own freedom. Meanwhile, McDonogh amassed a great fortune from their labor.

The Civil War caused the destruction of many of the great sugar plantations. Some were ransacked by occupying Federal troops (a few were burned). Many planters and their sons never returned from battle, or if they did, they had lost their spirit, health and fortune with the Southern cause.

But there were plantations that did survive, some by share cropping, some with hired hands and some reduced to smaller truck farms. There are still a few of the great houses left to view today. Many are restored and open to the public for touring. A few are still private homes. The tall columns and majestic oaks of these grand houses, are silent reminders of a unique heritage – the grandeur, traditions, luxuries, contradictions and burdens of a life far removed from today.

# New Orleans Jazz

When people think of New Orleans they think of Jazz. This unique art form was born in the city's exotic culture, during the 1890's, of roots that reach far back in the past. The slaves who came to America brought with them their music and dance from West Africa, often picking up influences from the West Indies, along the way. .Slavery, itself, produced chants, work songs and spirituals. These were songs of emotion - of love, anger, jealousy, longing, joy or despair.

During the 1800's, the slave dances at Congo Square became a weekly event, where, for a few hours, the music and dance of the African New Orleanians could be practiced and enjoyed. Slaves usually made their own instruments – skins stretched over sections of bamboo for drums, reed flutes, or banjos fashioned from gourds. Bones were used to beat the drums that accompanied the dances at Congo Square. The slaves often sang in a French *patois* (called *Creole*), or sang songs from Africa or the Caribbean.

Uniquely, in New Orleans, there was a large group of Free Persons of Color. They lived among, and considered themselves to be part of, Creole society, with a lifestyle and culture, totally separate from that of the slaves. Some were wealthy, and educated

*One of the leading personalities of Storyville was a State Legislator, who owned several saloons and was also the head of an oil company.*

their children in France. Some had mulatto or quadroon mothers and white fathers, who had provided for their education. Some came from the prominent families of Santo Dominican emigrés. Many studied classical music and played classical instruments, (like the white ladies and gentlemen of their day). Many performed professionally or taught music or dancing classes.

With the end of the Civil War, the new segregation laws saw no distinctions between these two black cultures, and their separate heritages were thrown together, influencing each other. The Creoles of color always remained a group somewhat apart - their unique culture and tradition of education, still passed on today.

It was during this period, after the War and Reconstruction, that Blues and Ragtime were born, and by the end of the century, they had become very popular throughout the country. New Orleans' love of chamber music, opera and dancing had kept music, a vital part of the city's culture and the old Creole and new Italian populations treasured their brass bands for parades and festive occasions.

But a new music was to emerge from a unique phenomenon – Storyville. (There is controversy as to whether Jazz was actually created in Storyville, or evolved out of the popular Ragtime music, and simply flourished and became famous as a separate art form there.)

Rampant corruption and crime in New Orleans had become so widespread by the 1880's, that there were hundreds of gambling halls and bars. Political pay-offs and corrupt police were allowing open prostitution, gambling and all types of crime. Desperate cries for reform led to an amazing plan – Alderman Sidney Story proposed the creation of two "districts," where all illegal activities could be contained, (and thus, controlled). What was created instead, was "a spectacle of legalized vice," that few visitors to New Orleans wanted to miss.

The District near the French Quarter was called Storyville, and became famous as *the* place of "entertainment for gentlemen," advertised, open and sanctioned. In just two blocks of Basin Street, there were at least 14 very fancy "sporting palaces," their landladies competing with elaborate decor, musical entertainment and originality of services offered. Behind the palaces, were blocks of the shacks of poor prostitutes.

It was in the bordellos and nightclubs of Storyville, that many black musicians found work. Each Madame wanted her house to have a "professor" to entertain her clients. Jelly Roll Morton was one of these professors – a Creole of color, and a very talented musician-composer, who became well known playing in Storyville.

Also in the first generation of New Orleans Jazzmen, were Louis Armstrong and Sidney Bechet. Armstrong was from a poor section of town and learned to play the cornet in the Colored Waifs' Home. He found a mentor in Papa Joe Oliver who was a cornetist and band leader (King Oliver).

Bechet was a Creole, like Morton, and a virtuoso on the clarinet. Entirely self taught, he began playing in Jazz bands at twelve, and never learned to read music.

There were many less known, but expert musicians, playing Ragtime, Blues and Jazz in the District and all over New Orleans. Also, groups of small boys formed bands,

*Jazz Funerals became popular in New Orleans, mostly as the final honoring of Jazz musicians. The band and "second liners" accompany the departed from the church to the cemetery, respectfully playing soulful dirges, to a slow and solemn drum beat. When the Jazz man is in his grave, and has been "set free," the mood is changed. As the procession leaves the cemetery, the music becomes spirited and lively and the second liners go into full swing.*

*New Orleans Jazz Greats : James Brown Humphrey, King Oliver, Jelly Roll Morton, Louis Armstrong, Sidney Bechet, Stalebread Lacombe, Jesse Hill Sweet Emma Barrett, Kid Ory, Johnny DeDroit, Papa Celestin, Bunk Johnson, Johnny Wiggs, David Lastie, Jack Dupree, Fats Pinchon, Sonny Boy Williamson, Huey Smith, Armand Hug, Louis Prima, Buddy Bolden, Fats Domino, Professor Longhair, Dr. John, James Booker, Ellis Marsalis, Allen Toussaint, Pete Fountain, Al Hirt, Irma Thomas, Aaron Neville, Ernie K-Doe, The Meters, Benny Spellman, Wynton Marsalis Terence Blanchard, Donald Harrison, Harry Connick, Jr., Branford Marsalis, Neville Brothers, Wild Tchoupitoulas*

performing on the sidewalks of the city for coins. These "spasm bands" often played on homemade instruments, learning music by ear - picking up the popular sounds coming from nightclubs and dancehalls.

Storyville operated, open and wild, for twenty years. In 1917, the U.S. Navy closed it down, to protect the sailors of WWI from exposure to "open vice." The entire District was then completely torn down.

Many of the musicians of Storyville left New Orleans in 1918, to find work further north. Jelly Roll Morton moved to Chicago. His complex compositions and progressive style of playing, showed operatic and Spanish elements, as well as Blues and Ragtime (giving insight into the beginnings of Jazz).

After playing on riverboats and perfecting his technique, Louis Armstrong found a place with King Oliver's band in Chicago in 1922. (His old mentor had moved north as well.) He spent the rest of his life traveling and playing, and helped to raise Jazz to an international art form. *Satchmo* became the world ambassador of Jazz.

Sidney Bechet left New Orleans in 1919 for Europe, where he became a celebrity musician, and a virtuoso on the saxophone, as well as the clarinet. He made his home in France, where he remained very popular.

At the same time that Storyville closed, a group of white New Orleans musicians, the Original Dixieland Jazz Band, recorded the first Jazz record in New York. A white style of Jazz improvisation, known as Dixieland, began to flourish in New Orleans, as well.

Jazz continued to thrive and evolve in New Orleans during the 1930's and '40's. After WW II, there came a major shift toward Rhythm and Blues. The rocking piano style and sweet voice of Fats Domino put Rhythm and Blues on the map. His music appealed to teenagers and the blue

collar and country folk alike. The other influential Rhythm and Blues man in New Orleans was Professor Longhair, who first introduced Carnival as a music theme.

Dr. John and James Booker both had popular hits during the 1950's. In the '60's, Allen Toussaint, an expert pianist, composed for such stars as Irma Thomas, Aaron Neville and Ernie K-Doe, among others. During the '70's, the Neville Brothers became a major group, adding AfroCaribbean facets to Rhythm and Blues.

It was also during the '70's that the Mardi Gras Indians combined with groups like the Neville Brothers and The Meters to make a new style of Carnival music. The Mardi Gras Indians are black neighborhood groups who have been dressing in fabulous, ornate "Indian" costumes since the 1870's. They work on creating their costumes all year, but traditionally dressed in them only on Mardi Gras and St. Joseph's Days. The new dimension of music was added to their *raison d'etre* and they have added much to the music of the city.

During the 1980's, a Jazz renaissance in New Orleans was led by a young trumpeter, Wynton Marsalis. His father, Ellis Marsalis, an accomplished composer pianist, was director of the Jazz Program at the Center for the Creative Arts. In addition to his own brilliantly musical sons (Wynton, Branford and Delfayo) he influenced students like Harry Connick, Jr, Terence Blanchard and Donald Harrison. These young Jazz musicians have been reaching back into the roots of their art form, as well as adding their own innovations to it.

Every spring, The Jazz and Heritage Festival is held in New Orleans, drawing a variety of musicians and enthusiasts for ten days of music and fun. Jazz is alive and well in the city of its birth.

*Storyville even had its own directory, The Bluebook, sold in hotels, railway stations and shops all over the city. It listed over 700 prostitutes, with large ads for individual Madames and "girls," as well as saloons, palaces, whiskey and cigars.*

# RUBENSTEINS

**Rubensteins** is a quality men's specialty store located in the heart of downtown New Orleans. Since 1924, we have offered world renowned clothing for men including designer lines: Brioni, Canali, Ermenegildo Zegna, Jack Victor, Ralph Lauren, Santoni Shoes and more.

The store is open Monday through Saturday, 10:00 am – 5:45 pm. Call the store at 504.581.6666 for more information or visit Rubensteins online at www.rubensteinsneworleans.com.

Rubensteins address is 102 St. Charles Ave., New Orleans, LA 70130 - at the corner of St. Charles and Canal "Where the Streetcar turns Uptown".

## Rubensteins Commemorative Streetcar Polo Shirts

A perfect gift, golf shirt, or everyday polo, these one of a kind, commemorative Streetcar Shirts are available for $49.50. They are available in sizes S–3XL and can only be found at Rubensteins in New Orleans! To order your Streetcar Shirt, please contact a Sales Associate at 504.581.6666 ext. 333.

10 Colors to Choose From!
Black, White, Light Blue, Slate Blue,
Emerald Green, Yellow,
Red, Tan, Navy &
Tangerine